www.icehockeyreview.co.uk

UK Hockey Yearbook 2018

WHO WON WHAT IN THE 2017/18 SEASON

Covering: Elite League, NIHL North & South, Scottish National League, Women's Leagues, British Para Ice Hockey League

and a Round Up of GB teams in the World Championships.

Interesting Books...
...Fascinating Subjects!

POSH UP NORTH
Publishing
www.poshupnorth.com

ISBN: 978-1-909643-28-4

First published in Great Britain in October 2018 by
Posh Up North Publishing
c/o 2 Beckenham Road, New Brighton CH45 2NZ

Front Cover Photo:
Team GB men's team celebrate winning the gold medal at the IIHF World Championships in Budapest in April 2018
(Photo by Dean Woolley – www.deanwoolley.co.uk)

Back Cover Photos:
Top: Minute's silence before the Widnes v Hull play off semi-final in memory of the Humboldt Broncos bus crash victims (by Rach Stork)

Left Column - Top to Bottom:	Right Column – Top to Bottom:
Cardiff Devils by Richard Davies	Belfast Giants by Helen Brabon
Sheffield Steeldogs by Peter Best	Sutton Sting by Christopher Rastall Photography
Basingstoke Bison by Grant King / 5 Hole Photography	Oxford City Stars by Paul Foster
Telford Tigers by Peter Best	Solent Devils by Kevin Slyfield
Widnes Wild by Geoff White	Swindon Wildcats by Ben Callaghan

Ice Hockey Review logo designed by John Milton
Mr Posh Up North logo designed by Steve Bainbridge

Statistics are taken from a variety of sources, including the EIHA website, Fixtures Live,
www.malcolm preen.co.uk and www.thesnl.co.uk.

Big thanks to all the team officials, reporters and photographers. Each author and photographer is acknowledged on their individual submissions.

As ever – if YOUR team isn't covered in the way you would have liked to see, it is probably because they didn't provide the information when invited to do so!

CONTENTS

This is actually my "cheerful" look!
Photo by Geoff White (www.gw-images.com)

INTRODUCTION
BY PAUL BREEZE

Well, here we all are again! To be completely honest, I hadn't actually planned on doing a UK Hockey Yearbook again this year.

I expanded the previous NIHL Yearbook in a bit of a rush last year to cover the EPL and, to a lesser extent, the Elite League in the wake of the news that Stewart Roberts had decided not to continue with his excellent Ice Hockey Annual.

But I had always said that the 2017 UK Hockey Yearbook was only ever going to be a one off and that I'd quite like to bow out myself after having produced the only UK publication EVER to cover Elite, EPL NIHL, Women's, Scottish and Para Ice Hockey in such minute detail.

But then, the end of the 2017/18 season approached, I was involved in the first ever Laidler Division play offs at Widnes, Team GB won the gold medal at the World Championships and I started to get those restless urges that you get in September when people go back to school or university - and like the woman gets in "Chocolat" when the wind blows.

Even though this is the ONLY book that is published about UK ice hockey, there is still a lot of competition out there. Most of the information contained herein – certainly the facts and figures and a lot of the photos - are readily available on the internet. That's ok as far as it goes but not all the information is gathered together in the same place in an easy to read format and, let's face it, if you haven't got access to the internet – or electricity, or whatever, you won't be able to find it. So at least we are "potential world catastrophe proof" in that respect - and this is a tangible item that you can easily give to your ice hockey fan friends and family members as Christmas or birthday presents!

Having said that, this edition is different from previous ones. A change in market conditions, ie fewer advertisers, rising print and distribution costs, people who (mystifyingly) don't buy books anymore mean that we are unable to carry on with the somewhat heavyweight "team by team" coverage with photos, reports and full stats. It is incredibly time consuming to put together and, while it is quite manageable if you are just dealing with 8 teams (ie ENL2N in 2011/12) or 20 teams (NIHL North in 11/12), it becomes a lot more cumbersome when you are looking at over 50 teams at some 3 or so pages per team.

Add to this the fact that I am a lot busier with rec hockey during the summer months than I ever used to be, the best option seemed to be change of format for this year and to focus on "who won what" in each section of UK hockey, with the result being a slightly sleeker publication which, at the end of the day, is cheaper for you to buy as well.

Hope you enjoy it!

Team GB – World Championships

Saturday 29th April
Hungary 2 – GB 3
P/Scores: 1-0, 0-0, 1-2
Penalty Shots 1-2

Dowd, Farmer
both 1+0, Brooks
Richardson 0+1

PS: O'Connor 2 –
Farmer 1

NM: Bowns 64.18
PS 5 faced 4 saved

Thursday 27th April
Italy 3 – Great Britain 4
P/Scores: 2-2, 0-1, 1-1

Perlini 2+0, O'Connor
1+1, Dowd 1+0,
Richardson Brook,
Swindlehurst, Lee all 0+1

NM: Bowns 60.00 36s/3

Tuesday 25th April
Great Britain 5 –
Poland 3
P/Scores: 2-1, 0-3, 3-0

Perlini 1+1, Shields1+1,
Phillips, Brooks
O'Connor all 1+0,
Farmer 0+2, Lachowicz,
Betteridge, Richardson,
Lee, Dowd, Hammond
all 0+1

NM: Bowns 60.00 39s/3

Monday 24th April
Kazakhstan 6 – GB 1
P/Scores: 1-1, 2-0, 3-0

Ferrara 1+0, Brooks 0+1

NM: Bowns 44.55 33s/5
Whistle 14.05 9s/1

Saturday 22nd April
GB 3 – Slovenia 1
P/Scores: 1-1, 1-0, 1-0

Perlini 1+1, O'Connor
1+1, Dowd 1+0,
Hammond & Shields 0+1

NM Bowns 60.00 35s/1g

Photos from top:

*Brett Perlini and Colin
Shields celebrate a goal
against Slovenia,*

*GB netminder Ben Bowns
makes an important save
in the last game against
Hungary*

Gold medal celebrations.

(photos by Dean Woolley)

Back to Back Golds For Team GB Men
By Paul Breeze

Following from the previous year's sensational Gold medal winning display in Belfast, and promotion back up to Division 1 Group A for the first time since 2013, Team GB head coach Peter Russell's immediate objective had been merely to stay up – and work towards consolidating at this level of world hockey over future years.

The squad saw 8 new caps, the most notable being Brett Perlini - son of the British League era import Fred Perlini and brother of Brendan Perlini who is currently playing in the NHL for the Arizona Coyotes - and who, while having been born in Canada, played his early years hockey at Guildford and thus qualified as a GB player. In fact 20 of the 22 man squad was GB born so this team really was a home-grown team.

The tournament started well for Team GB with a 3-1 win over Slovenia but they were brought down to earth with a bump in the next game against Kazakhstan where they came out on the wrong end of a 6-1 defeat. Things got back on track with a 5-3 win over Poland but then a dramatic - and, to be honest, slightly unexpected - 3-4 win over Italy put things in a whole new light.

Kazakhstan had lost 3-0 to Italy and 5-3 to Slovenia whereas hosts Hungary, having lost to Kazakhstan in their opening game, had won all three games since. This meant that the whole outcome of the group would be decided in the final game between Hungary and Team GB. Things were so close that if Hungary won the game they would be promoted along with Kazakhstan but Team GB only needed a single point out of the game, ie to be drawing at the of 60 minutes, to secure promotion to the top flight of world hockey for the first time since 1994.

The big game started badly for Team GB as Hungary took the lead in the 4th minute. The second period was goal-less but a second goal for the hosts early in the third period left GB with a lot to do.

Paul Swindlehurst and Brett Perlini had chances to close the gap before Robert Dowd spun on the spot and fired the puck through traffic on a rebound to reduce the arrears at 50:55.

Hungary were awarded a penalty shot with just 3 minutes to go which would have meant the end of GB promotion hopes but netminder Ben Bowns saved his second PS of the tournament as he denied Janos Hari.

With just 57 seconds left of the game, coach Russell pulled off netminder Bowns in favour of an extra attacker and the GB team laid siege to the Hungarian goal. Then with 15 seconds remaining, Robert Farmer wriggled free from his marker and his low shot slid under the Hungarian netminder to secure GB the point they needed.

A goal-less period of overtime followed and then penalty shots were needed to decide the game, which GB won 2-1. This result meant that GB finished top of the group and won the gold medal and Italy finished in second to win the silver medal. Both teams were promoted to the top division of world ice hockey for the 2019 World Championships.

Great Britain Team Photo - WC 2018 (Photo by Dean Woolley)
Back Row: Zach Sullivan, Stephen Lee, Brendan Brooks, Luke Ferrara, Liam Kirk, Ollie Betteridge
Middle Row: Mairi MacPhail (Team Physio), Steve Small (Equipment Manager), Jason Ellery (Equipment Manager), Ben Davies, Robert Farmer, Dallas Erhardt, Paul Swindlehurst, David Philips, Brett Perlini, Mike Hammond, Ben O'Connor, Andy Buxton (General Manager), Matt Robbins (Team Doctor), Nikki Sherlock (Team Physio).
Front Row: Jackson Whistle, Robert Lachowicz, Mark Richardson, Corey Neilson (Asst Coach), Jonathan Phiips, Peter Russell (Head Coach), Robert Dowd, Adam Keefe (Asst Coach), Matt Myers, Colin Shields, Ben Bowns.

World Championships Division I Group A - 22nd to 29th April 2018, Budapest

TEAM GB PLAYER STATISTICS - WC 2018

No	Name	L/R	Ht	Wt	DoB	Team	Gp	G	A	Pts	PIM
			Netminders								
1*	WHISTLE Jackson	L	6'1"	192	9/6/95	BEL	5	0	0	0	0
30	BOWNS Ben	R	6'0"	179	21/191	CAR	5	0	0	0	0
			Defencemen								
2*	EHRHARDT Dallas	L	6'4"	225	31/7/92	MAN	5	0	1	1	8
4	LEE Stephen	R	6'0"	198	1/10/90	NOT	5	0	2	2	4
6*	SULLIVAN Zach	R	5'9"	181	14/7/94	BHC	5	0	0	0	0
13	PHILLIPS David	R	6'3"	187	14/8/87	SHE	5	0	0	0	6
17	RICHARDSON Mark	R	6'0"	194	3/10/86	CAR	5	0	3	3	2
23	SWINDLEHURST Paul	L	6'4"	198	25/5/93	MAN	5	0	1	1	4
28	OCONNOR Ben	L	6'1"	187	21/12/88	SHE	5	4	2	6	2
			Forwards								
5	DAVIES Benjamin	R	5'8"	165	18/1/91	GUI	5	0	0	0	4
7	LACHOWICZ Robert	L	5'10"	168	8/2/90	NOT	5	0	1	1	0
8	MYERS Matthew	R	6'2"	205	6/11/84	CAR	5	0	0	0	4
9*	PERLINI Brett	L	6'2"	201	14/6/90	NOT	5	4	2	6	2
10	FARMER Robert	L	6'3"	207	21/3/91	NOT	5	1	2	3	0
12	DOWD Robert	R	5'10"	176	26/5/88	SHE	5	3	1	4	0
14*	KIRK Liam	L	6'0"	159	3/1/00	SHE	5	0	0	0	0
18*	BETTERIDGE Oliver	R	5'11"	176	16/1/96	NOT	5	0	1	1	0
19	SHIELDS Colin	R	5'11"	181	27/1/80	BEL	5	1	2	3	0
20	PHILLIPS Jonathan	R	5'9"	179	14/7/82	SHE	5	1	0	1	2
21*	HAMMOND Mike	R	5'10"	181	21/2/90	MAN	5	0	2	2	0
24	BROOKS Brendan	L	5'9"	185	26/11/78	BHC	5	1	3	4	2
27*	FERRARA Luke	R	5'11"	196	7/6/93	COV	5	1	0	1	0

Team GB Netminder Statistics – WC 2018

	GP	Mins	GA	SVS	SOG	%SVS	GAA
Ben Bowns	5	290:13:00	14	159	173	91.91	2.89
Jackson Whistle	5	14:05	1	8	9	88.89	4.26

Team GB Coaching Staff – WC 2018

Function	Name	Citizenship	Date of Birth
Head Coach	RUSSELL Peter	GBR	20 Jun 1974
Assistant Coach	NEILSON Corey	GBR	22 Aug 1976
Assistant Coach	KEEFE Adam	CAN	26 Apr 1984
General Manager	BUXTON Andy	GBR	22 Oct 1965
Equipment Manager	ELLERY Jason	GBR	20 May 1970
Physiotherapist	SHERLOCK Nikki	GBR	22 Dec 1973

Team GB – World Championships

World Championships Division I Group A
22nd to 29th April 2018, Budapest, Hungary

Final Group Table

Pos	Team	Pld	W	OTW	OTL	L	GF	GA	GD	Pts	Result
1	Great Britain	5	3	1	0	1	16	15	1	11	Promoted
2	Italy	5	3	0	0	2	15	11	4	9	Promoted
3	Kazakhstan	5	3	0	0	2	18	10	8	9	
4	Hungary	5	2	0	1	2	9	14	-5	7	
5	Slovenia	5	2	0	0	3	15	15	0	6	
6	Poland	5	1	0	0	4	11	19	-8	3	Relegated

Top Points Scorers – WC Div 1 Group A 2018

Player	Team	GP	G	A	Pts	PIM	POS
Roman Starchenko	KAZ	5	6	2	8	4	F
Miha Verlič	SLO	5	3	4	7	2	F
Ben O'Connor	GBR	5	4	2	6	2	D
Brett Perlini	GBR	5	4	2	6	2	F
Jan Urbas	HUN	5	3	3	6	0	F
Evgeni Rymarev	KAZ	5	2	4	6	2	F
Ivan Deluca	ITA	5	1	5	6	2	F
Balázs Sebők	HUN	5	3	2	5	2	F
Aron Chmielewski	POL	5	2	3	5	2	F
Robert Dowd	GBR	5	3	1	4	0	F

Top Netminders – WC Div 1 Group A 2018

Netminder	Team	TOI	GA	GAA	SA	Sv%	SO
Henrik Karlsson	KAZ	300:00:00	10	2	159	93.71	1
Ádám Vay	HUN	304:46:00	13	2.56	189	93.12	0
Marco De Filippo	ITA	157:33:00	5	1.9	66	92.42	0
Ben Bowns	GBR	290:13:00	14	2.89	173	91.91	0
Przemysław Odrobny	POL	159:18:00	9	3.39	93	90.32	0

Key: TOI = Time on Ice (minutes:seconds); SA = Shots Against; GA = Goals Against; GAA = Goals Against Average; Sv% = Save Percentage; SO = Shutouts

Note: Top only the five goaltenders, based on save percentage, who have played at least 40% of their team's minutes are listed .

Team GB – World Championships

Women's World Championships Division II Group A
31st March to 6th April 2018, Maribor, Slovenia

Final Group Table

Pos	Team	Pld	W	OTW	OTL	L	GF	GA	GD	Pts
1	Netherlands	5	5	0	0	0	24	3	+21	15
2	Great Britain	5	4	0	0	1	17	7	+10	12
3	North Korea	5	3	0	0	2	14	15	−1	9
4	Australia	5	2	0	0	3	10	17	−7	6
5	Slovenia	5	1	0	0	4	14	15	−1	3
6	Mexico	5	0	0	0	5	3	25	−22	0

Playing Statistics

No	Name	Pos	GP	G	A	PTS	PIM	+/-	GWG	PPG	SHG	SOG	SG%
1	JACKSON Nicole	GK	5	0	0	0	0		0	0	0	0	0.00
2	SCOON Bethany	D	5	0	0	0	2	0	0	0	0	4	0.00
3	TAYLOR Angela	F	5	4	2	6	4	+4	2	0	0	21	19.05
4	TRAILL Casey	F	5	0	0	0	0	0	0	0	0	2	0.00
5	SUMMERS Lauren	D	5	0	0	0	0	+1	0	0	0	1	0.00
6	HENRY Katie	F	5	2	3	5	2	+6	1	1	0	16	12.50
7	FARMAN Georgina	F	5	1	0	1	4	+2	0	0	0	7	14.29
8	HUTCHINSON Sarah	D	5	0	2	2	2	+3	0	0	0	4	0.00
9	BLOOM Jodie-Leigh	F	5	0	1	1	0	0	0	0	0	18	0.00
11	GALE Katherine	F	5	0	2	2	2	+2	0	0	0	13	0.00
12	ADAMS Louise	F	5	1	0	1	0	0	0	0	0	21	4.76
13	CORNFORD Holly	D	5	0	1	1	0	+2	0	0	0	1	0.00
14	GANNEY Leanne	F	5	3	2	5	2	+5	0	0	0	21	14.29
15	HILL Bethany	D	5	2	2	4	2	+5	0	0	0	19	10.53
16	ALLEN Saffron	F	5	1	3	4	4	+3	0	1	0	8	12.50
17	HERBERT Sophie	F	5	1	1	2	6	+5	0	0	0	9	11.11
18	ASHTON Clara	F	5	1	0	1	2	0	0	0	0	3	33.33
19	LANE Kimberley	F	5	1	3	4	2	+3	1	1	0	5	20.00
21	LEWIS Verity	D	5	0	1	1	4	+1	0	0	0	2	0.00
23	EMERY Ali	D	5	0	0	0	2	+3	0	0	0	3	0.00
24	CULSHAW Abigail	F	5	0	0	0	0	0	0	0	0	2	0.00
25	BOLWELL Samantha	GK	5	0	0	0	0		0	0	0	0	0.00

Goalkeeping Statistics

No	Name	GPT	GKD	GPI	MIP	MIP%	GA	SVS	SOG	SVS%	GAA	SO	W	L
1	JACKSON Nicole	5	5	3	180:00	60.00	6	52	58	89.66	2.00	0	2	1
25	BOLWELL Samantha	5	5	2	120:00	40.00	1	35	36	97.22	0.50	1	2	0

LEGEND					
A	Assists	D	Defence	F	Forward
G	Goals	GA	Goals against	GA	Goals against as average per 60 minutes
GK	Goalkeeper	GKD	Goalkeeper dressed	GP	Number of games played
GPI	Games played indeed	GPT	Number of games played by team	GWG	Game winning goals
L	Number of games lost	MIP	Minutes and seconds played	MIP%	MIP as percentage
No	Jersey number	PIM	Penalties in minutes	Pos	Position on team
PPG	Power play goals	PTS	Points	SG%	Percentage of goals from total shots
SHG	Shorthanded goals	SO	Shutouts	SOG	Shots on goal
SVS	Saves	SVS%	SVS as percentage of total SOG	W	Number of games won
+/-	Plus/minus net				

Team GB – World Championships

6th April 2018:
Netherlands 4 - Team GB 0
Period Scores:
0-0, 3-0, 1-0

4th April 2018:
Slovenia 1 –
Team GB 4
Period Scores:
0-1, 0-2, 1-1
GB Scorers: Hill 1+0,
Henry 1+1, Taylor 1+1,
Herbert 1+0, Cornford,
Gale, Alley, Hutchinson
0+1

3rd April 2018:
Team GB 5 – Mexico 0
Period Scores:
1-0, 2-0, 2-0
GB Scorers: Lane,
Ashton, Allen, Henry,
Adams 1+0
Hill 0+2, Taylor,
Hutchinson, Ganney,
Gale, Bloom all 0+1

1st April 2018:
Team GB 3 –
North Korea 1
Period Scores:
1-0, 1-1, 1-0
GB Scorers: Ganney
1+0, Taylor 1+0, Farman
1+0, Lane , Henry 0+2,
Herbert, Allen 0+1

31st March 2018:
Team GB 5 –
Australia 1
Period Scores:
0-0, 0-1, 5-0
GB Scorers: Ganney
2+1, Taylor 2+0, Hill 1+0,
Lewis, Allen, Lane 0+1

Photos from top:

*Katherine Gale and
Jodie Bloom in action v
Australia*

Louise Adams

CJ Ashton

*Sarah Hutchinson v PK
Korea*

*Face off Team GB v
Mexico*

Samantha Bolwell

Georgina Farman

*Match action from Team
GB v Netherlands*

(Photos by Rob Hutchinson and Lois Tomlinson)

Great Britain Women's Team Photo – WC 2018, Slovenia (Photo by Rob Hutchinson)

Back row(l to r): CJ Ashton, Casey Trail, Lauren Summers, Angela Taylor, Sam Bolwell, Kim Lane, Jodie Bloom, Beth Scoon, Sarah, Nicole, Holly Cornford.

Front Row (l to): Katherine Gale, Abigail Culshaw, Saffron Allen, Sophie Herbert, Verity Lewis, Leanne Ganney, Katie Henry, Georgina Farman, Beth Hill, Louise Adams, Ali Emery.

GB Women's Team

The GB women's team went one better than they did the previous year in Korea but, at the end of the week, winning the silver medal almost came as a disappointment considering how the tournament had gone.

After a nervy start against Australia in their opening game - where they actually trailed 0-1 after two periods before moving up a gear to end up 5-1 winners - they swept past North Korea, Mexico and hosts Slovenia without ever falling behind again.

This set up a tantalising "winner takes all" deciding game against the Netherlands team that had finished above them last time around in Korea to decide who would take the gold meal and win promotion to Division 1. The Dutch had also won all 4 of their group games in Maribor, scoring an impressive 20 goals and conceding just 3, so it was not going to be an easy game.

After a tense and goal-less first period, the Dutch took control of the game with 3 goals in the second and added a fourth right at the start of the third to kill off the match. The GB girls worked hard throughout but had difficulty maintaining pressure on the NL net and were caught out in defence on breakaways.

It's always nice to win a medal - and silver is definitely better than bronze. With no relegation this year from the upper tier, the Team GB women will be well placed to go one better in the 2019 World Championships.

Under 18s World Championships Division II Group A
31st March to 6th April 2018, Tallin, Estonia

Final Group Table

Pos	Team	Pld	W	OTW	OTL	L	GF	GA	GD	Pts
1	Great Britain	5	4	0	0	1	26	15	+11	12
2	Lithuania	5	4	0	0	1	22	8	+14	12
3	Poland	5	3	1	0	1	32	11	+21	11
4	Korea	5	2	0	0	3	12	14	-2	6
5	Estonia	5	1	0	1	3	17	21	-4	4
6	Australia	5	0	0	0	5	4	44	-40	0

Playing Statistics

No	Name	Pos	GP	G	A	PTS	PIM	+/-	GWG	PPG	SHG	SOG	SG%
1	DAVIES Lewis	GK	5	0	0	0	0		0	0	0	0	0.00
2	BRADLEY Edward	D	5	1	3	4	4	+8	0	0	0	9	11.11
3	HAZELDINE Joseph	D	5	0	2	2	4	+3	0	0	0	6	0.00
4	BURNETT Callum	D	5	0	0	0	2	0	0	0	0	7	0.00
5	COCHRANE Reece	D	5	1	0	1	2	+6	0	0	0	2	50.00
6	GRIFFIN Jordan	D	5	0	2	2	2	+2	0	0	0	0	0.00
7	HODGKINSON Joshua	D	5	0	0	0	0	+2	0	0	0	0	0.00
8	SOLDER Ben	D	5	1	3	4	6	+6	0	0	0	12	8.33
9	RUSSELL Samuel	D	5	0	0	0	0	+2	0	0	0	0	0.00
11	BROWN Kieran	F	5	4	4	8	8	+5	1	0	0	15	26.67
12	BUESA Jordan	F	5	3	1	4	2	+5	1	0	1	17	17.65
14	KIRK Liam	F	5	4	3	7	2	+4	2	0	1	33	12.12
15	STRANGEWAY Aidan	D	5	0	1	1	2	0	0	0	0	1	0.00
16	NEILSON Cade	F	5	2	4	6	6	+6	0	0	1	16	12.50
17	ALDERSON Mason	F	5	6	3	9	2	+9	0	1	0	18	33.33
18	KROGH Richard	F	5	2	2	4	4	+2	0	2	0	18	11.11
19	LARKIN Patrick	F	5	1	2	3	2	+2	0	0	0	9	11.11
20	KERLIN William	GK	5	0	0	0	0		0	0	0	0	0.00
21	ULRICK Finlay	F	5	1	5	6	2	+3	0	0	0	17	5.88
22	ROBERTSON Calum	F	2	0	2	2	0	+3	0	0	2	2	0.00
23	MITCHELL-KING Austin	F	5	0	1	1	0	+1	0	0	0	4	0.00
24	ENGLISH Lewis	F	5	0	0	0	0	-1	0	0	0	1	0.00

Goalkeeping Statistics

No	Name	GPT	GKD	GPI	MIP	MIP%	GA	SVS	SOG	SVS%	GAA	SO	W	L
1	DAVIES Lewis	5	5	1	60:00	20.03	2	21	23	91.30	2.00	0	1	0
20	KERLIN William	5	5	4	239:29	79.97	13	90	103	87.38	3.26	0	3	1

LEGEND					
A	Assists	D	Defence	F	Forward
G	Goals	GA	Goals against	GAA	Goals against as average per 60 minutes
GK	Goalkeeper	GKD	Goalkeeper dressed	GP	Number of games played
GPI	Games played indeed	GPT	Number of games played by team	GWG	Game winning goals
L	Number of games lost	MIP	Minutes and seconds played	MIP%	MIP as percentage
No	Jersey number	PIM	Penalties in minutes	Pos	Position on team
PPG	Power play goals	PTS	Points	SG%	Percentage of goals from total shots
SHG	Shorthanded goals	SO	Shutouts	SOG	Shots on goal
SVS	Saves	SVS%	SVS as percentage of total SOG	W	Number of games won
+/-	Plus/minus net				

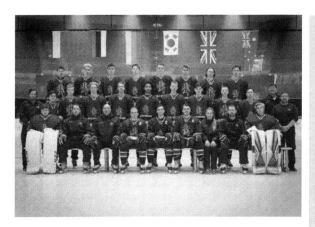

7th April 2018
Korea 3 – GB U18 4
Period Scores:
0-2, 3-1, 0-1

GB Scorers:
Bradley 1+1, Kirk 1+1,
Finlay 1+0, Krogh 1+0,
Brown, Buesa,
Strangeway all 0+1

6th April 2018
GB U18 3 – Lithuania 2
Period Scores:
1-0, 2-2, 0-0

GB Scorers:
Solder 1+1, Alderson
1+0, Kirk 1+0, Bradley,
Ulrick, Hazeldine, Larkin,
all 0+1

4th April 2018
Poland 5 – GB U18 4
Period Scores:
3-2, 0-2, 2-0

GB Scorers:
Alderson 2+1, Brown
1+0, Cochrane 1+0,
Bradley, Solder, Kirk
Ulrick, Neilson, Mitchell-
King all 0+1

2nd April 2018
GB 9 – Australia 2
Period Scores:
2-1, 5-1, 2-0

GB Scorers:
Brown 3+2, Kirk 2+1,
Neilson 2+1, Alderson
1+2, Buesa 1+0, Griffin
0+2, Solder, Hazeldine,
Krogh, Larkin, Robertson
all 0+1

1st April 2018
Estonia 3 - GB U18 6
Period Scores:
0-4, 3-2, 0-0

GB Scorers:
Neilson 0+2, Krogh 1+1,
Robertson 0+1, Brown
0+1, Alderson 2+0,
Buesa 2+0, Larkin 1+0

GB Under 18 Team

The Under 18 World Championships saw Team GB playing in Division IIA in Tallinn, Estonia, against Lithuania, Poland, Australia, South Korea and the host nation. They beat Estonia 3-6 in their opening game and then saw off Australia 9-2.

A narrow 5-4 defeat to Poland followed which might have scuppered their chances of securing the gold medal but Team GB bounced back with a 3-2 win over Lithuania which would turn out to be very significant in the final standings.

They played potential banana skin South Korea in their last group game and led 0-3 early in the second period but three straight goals saw them pegged back to 3-3 by the mid-point of the game.

A short handed goal from Liam Kirk after just 43 seconds of the third period edged GB back in front and there they stayed until the final buzzer.

The win saw them finish level on points with Lithuania but GB took the gold medal by virtue of their 3-2 win in the game between the two teams.

Elite League

Elite League action between the two new teams – Milton Keynes Lightning v Guildford Flames.
(Photo by Melissa Dickens / MJD Photography - www.mjdphoto.biz)

The Elite League was expanded to twelve teams for the 2017/18 season with the addition of two former EPL teams – Guildford Flames and Milton Keynes Lightning.

This enabled the formation of a new third conference – the Patton Conference - named after Peter Patton, the former Princes club player and pioneering administrator who oversaw the spread of the sport in Britain and Europe in the early 1900s, and who was involved in the setting up of both the IIHF in 1908 and the BIHA in 1913.

The new 3-conference system was mainly geographical to cut down on travelling costs for the teams and saw the 4 Scottish teams contest the Gardiner Conference among themselves with the remaining 8 teams (6 English, 1 Welsh and 1 Northern Irish) being split into two conferences of 4, based loosely around ability.

The teams played an interlocking system meeting the other 3 sides in their own conference eight times overall (ie 24 games) and the eight teams from the other two conferences four times in all (32 games) for a 56 games overall Elite League regular season.

For anybody with a particularly long hockey memory, this arrangement reminds me of the three-group system that was put in place with the first British League season of 1982/83 which saw Dundee Rockets, Durham Wasps and Altrincham Aces become champions of Sections A, B & C respectively – but I digress…

To understand the league tables better, it is worth mentioning that two points were awarded for a win and one for an overtime defeat or penalty shootout defeat.

Overtime was played as five minutes of three-on-three hockey and ended immediately if a goal is scored. The team that had the most points at the end of the regular season was declared champion.

Elite League

Elite League – Final Standings 2017/19

TEAM	GP	RW	W	L	OTL	SOL	PTS	PCT	GF	GA	PIM
Cardiff Devils	56	37	41	12	1	2	85	0.759	234	149	797
Manchester Storm	56	28	35	16	3	2	75	0.67	216	169	1102
Sheffield Steelers	56	32	34	19	2	1	71	0.634	217	140	1027
Nottingham Panthers	56	25	33	18	2	3	71	0.634	203	177	839
Belfast Giants	56	30	34	20	2	0	70	0.625	227	200	1195
Guildford Flames	56	27	30	17	5	4	69	0.616	215	173	746
Fife Flyers	56	27	33	21	1	1	68	0.607	218	172	639
Coventry Blaze	56	22	25	26	4	1	55	0.491	189	186	1076
Braehead Clan	56	24	24	26	5	1	54	0.482	161	186	823
Dundee Stars	56	16	22	30	3	1	48	0.429	167	233	755
M Keynes Lightning	56	16	20	34	1	1	42	0.375	180	229	1054
Edinburgh Capitals	56	5	5	50	0	1	11	0.098	118	331	690

Erhardt Conference – Final Standings 2017/18

TEAM	GP	RW	W	L	OTL	SOL	PTS	PCT	GF	GA	PIM
Cardiff Devils	24	13	15	7	0	2	32	.625	91	69	367
Belfast Giants	24	11	13	9	2	0	28	.500	75	83	608
Sheffield Steelers	24	10	10	12	1	1	22	.417	68	62	563
Nottingham Panthers	24	8	10	14	0	0	20	.396	77	97	446

Gardiner Conference – Final Standings 2017/18

TEAM	GP	RW	W	L	OTL	SOL	PTS	PCT	GF	GA	PIM
Fife Flyers	24	17	19	3	1	1	40	.792	123	56	327
Braehead Clan	24	14	14	8	1	1	30	.583	85	71	329
Dundee Stars	24	9	13	10	1	0	27	.479	83	96	357
Edinburgh Capitals	24	2	2	21	0	1	5	.083	59	127	303

Patton Conference – Final Standings 2017/18

TEAM	GP	RW	W	L	OTL	SOL	PTS	PCT	GF	GA	PIM
Manchester Storm	24	13	15	8	1	0	31	.604	90	71	486
Guildford Flames	24	12	13	6	2	3	31	.521	90	72	283
Coventry Blaze	24	11	12	11	1	0	25	.500	87	91	552
Milton K Lightning	24	4	8	15	0	1	17	.292	68	101	481

According to the Elite League website, the regulations regarding numbers of players for the 2017/18 season was as follows:

"The maximum bench roster for the 2017/18 season will be set at 19 plus up to three British trained players born in 1994 or later. The initial 19 skaters comprises of a maximum of 14 import players, with the league no longer requiring an 11+3 split where the 'three' imports would need to be exempt from requiring a work permit."

Elite League

Above: Manchester Storm receive the Patton Conference trophy in its inaugural season.
(All Storm photos by Mark Ferriss – All Sports Photography)

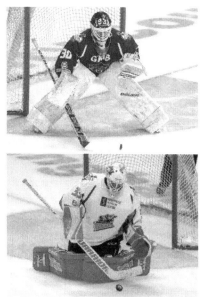

Manchester Storm's Mike Hammond was the top points scorer for the Elite League with 83 points in 56 games.

Nottingham Panthers' netminder Patrick Galbraith (top) ended up with the highest Save % for the Elite League season while Ervins Mustukovs of Sheffield Steelers (above) had the best GAA. (Both photos by Richard Davies www.smugmug.chud.com)

Elite League – Leading Points Scorers 2017/18

PLAYER	TEAM	GP	G	A	PTS	PIM	PP	PPA	SH	SHA	GWG
Hammond, Mike	MAN	56	32	51	83	10	6	19	1	2	2
Dunbar, John	GUI	55	22	59	81	34	4	24	1	2	4
Beca, Matt	MAN	56	24	51	75	14	7	16	2	1	4
Martin, Joey	CAR	55	27	46	73	26	8	21	1	0	5
Connolly, Brendan	BEL	53	27	46	73	154	5	13	0	0	3
Sylvestre, Sebastien	BEL	54	32	40	72	152	6	10	0	0	2
Byers, Dane	MAN	55	24	46	70	107	7	15	2	2	3
Moffatt, Luke	MAN	56	34	32	66	73	8	6	2	0	7
Reddick, Kruise	GUI	54	27	39	66	36	8	15	3	2	2
Vallerand, Marc-Olivier	COV	48	34	31	65	145	7	7	1	1	4

Key: GP = Games Played, G = Goals, A = Assists, PTS = Points scored (ie goals + assists), PIM = Penalties In Minutes, PP = Powerplay Goals, PPA = Powerplay Assists, SH = Short Handed Goals, SHA = Short Handed Assists, GWG = Game Winning Goal

Elite League – Top Netminders By Save %

NAME	TEAM	GP	MIN	W	L	SO	GA	GAA	SV	SV%
Bowns, Ben	CAR	51	2937:01:00	38	10	6	119	2.43	1228	91.2
Clemente, Mike	MAN	55	3323:03:00	35	15	3	156	2.82	1530	90.7
Mustukovs, Ervins	SHF	53	3097:39:00	31	19	9	122	2.36	1368	91.8
Iles, Andy	FIF	42	2369:49:00	28	10	2	106	2.68	1115	91.3
Whistle, Jackson	BEL	44	2575:33:00	27	15	0	145	3.38	1236	89.5
Carrozzi, Chris	GUI	43	2589:09:00	25	13	3	119	2.76	1124	90.4
Nastiuk, Kevin	COV	56	3269:35:00	25	26	1	170	3.12	1524	90
Nie, Ryan	BRA	53	3173:17:00	23	26	1	163	3.08	1525	90.3
Fullerton, Travis	DUN	54	3164:40:00	22	29	1	205	3.89	1539	88.2
Galbraith, Patrick	NOT	27	1445:25:00	19	8	2	62	2.57	752	92.4

Elite League - Top Netminders by Goals Against Average

NAME	TEAM	GP	MIN	W	L	SO	GA	GAA	SV	SV%
Mustukovs, Erv	SHF	53	3097:39:00	31	19	9	122	2.36	1368	91.8
Bowns, Ben	CAR	51	2937:01:00	38	10	6	119	2.43	1228	91.2
Galbraith, Patrick	NOT	27	1445:25:00	19	8	2	62	2.57	752	92.4
Iles, Andy	FIF	42	2369:49:00	28	10	2	106	2.68	1115	91.3
Carrozzi, Chris	GUI	43	2589:09:00	25	13	3	119	2.76	1124	90.4
Clemente, Mike	MAN	55	3323:03:00	35	15	3	156	2.82	1530	90.7
Nie, Ryan	BRA	53	3173:17:00	23	26	1	163	3.08	1525	90.3
Nastiuk, Kevin	COV	56	3269:35:00	25	26	1	170	3.12	1524	90
Garnett, Michael	NOT	33	1822:06:00	14	10	0	101	3.33	841	89.3
Whistle, Jackson	BEL	44	2575:33:00	27	15	0	145	3.38	1236	89.5

Elite League

Fife Flyers celebrate the 2017/18 Gardiner Conference title win.
(Photo by Fife Flyers Official Facebook Page)

Above left: Cardiff Devils captain Jake Morissette and Director Neil Francis with the Erhardt Conference trophy.
Above Right: Devils' Alternate Captain Mark Richardson holds aloft the Elite League trophy.
(Both photos by Helen Brabon – www.helenbrabonphotography.co.uk)

Elite League

Belfast Giants celebrate beating Cardiff Devils on their own ice to win the 2018 Challenge Cup final.
(Photo by Helen Brabon – www.helenbrabonphotography.co.uk)

ELITE LEAGUE CHALLENGE CUP

Cup Final - 4th March 2018 at Ice Arena Wales: Cardiff Devils 3 - Belfast Giants 6
P/Scores: 1-0, 1-3, 1-3 / SOG: Devils 30 – Giants 25 / PIM: Devils 10 – Giants 12

Elite League Challenge Cup – Semi Finals

1st Leg – 31st Jan 2018	2nd Leg – 7th Feb 2018	Aggregate Score
Panthers 1 - Giants 5	Giants 7 – Panthers 6	Belfast win 12-7
Steelers 6 - Cardiff Devils 2	Devils 7 – Steelers 1	Cardiff win 9-7

Qualifying Groups

Group A	GP	W	L	OTL	SOL	GF	GA	PIM	PTS
Sheffield Steelers	10	9	1	0	0	44	27	122	18
Nottingham Panthers	10	4	6	0	0	37	36	100	8
Manchester Storm	6	2	4	0	0	20	23	99	4
Braehead Clan	6	1	4	1	0	16	25	57	3
Group B	**GP**	**W**	**L**	**OTL**	**SOL**	**GF**	**GA**	**PIM**	**PTS**
Belfast Giants	11	8	1	0	1	56	33	143	18
Fife Flyers	8	3	4	0	0	27	32	97	7
Dundee Stars	8	3	5	0	0	23	37	102	6
Edinburgh Capitals	6	2	3	0	1	21	27	101	5
Group C	**GP**	**W**	**L**	**OTL**	**SOL**	**GF**	**GA**	**PIM**	**PTS**
Milton Keynes Lightning	8	6	2	0	0	29	23	182	12
Cardiff Devils	11	5	4	1	0	44	40	184	12
Guildford Flames	8	3	3	0	1	27	30	124	8
Coventry Blaze	6	1	4	1	0	18	29	147	3

Elite League

ELITE LEAGUE PLAY OFF WEEKEND
National Ice Centre, Nottingham

Final: CARDIFF DEVILS 3 SHEFFIELD STEELERS 1

Cardiff Devils made history as they won their first ever play-off title in Elite League history and first since the old Super League era in 1999.

Matt Pope, Andrew Hotham and Jake Morissette were the history makers as Andrew Lord's men got their revenge after missing out in a dramatic 6-5 double overtime loss last year.

While this final perhaps wasn't as high tempo and manic as the meeting 12 months ago, it was every bit as tense as Devils needed an empty net to be sure of silverware.

While there were plenty of chances throughout a fairly hectic first period, both teams had nothing to show for their efforts.

Cardiff's first chance come a few minutes later when a scramble kicked off in front of Ervins Mustukovs' crease, with Joey Haddad getting a touch on it, but no killer finish.

Joey Martin was denied for the Devils after the Steelers' goalie coughed up a rebound after Josh Batch had tested him.

A cross ice pass from the left found Justin Faryna on the doorstep, but unable to convert as Mustukovs read it to deny him.

Steelers had a couple of half decent chances when Mark Matheson and Tim Wallace both tried efforts on Bowns, that were stopped.

The league champions open the door after 25 minutes when Joey Martin played assist maker for Matt Pope, who lashed a blue line shot over Mustukovs' shoulder.

Ben O'Connor tried to level, but again found Bowns in top form, while Tyson Strachan, up the other end, tried a one-timer that was deflected over by the Sheffield netminder.

Steelers had arguably their best chance of the game when the puck bounced in the direction of Robert Dowd, free in the centre, but his effort was stopped by Cardiff's stopper.

Then the second came and it was Devils who were celebrating again as Andrew Hotham cut in from the right and delivered a fabulous shot that flew over Mustukovs' blocker and into the net.

Layne Ulmer almost added a third when his shot from outside the crease, from Faryna's pass saw Sheffield's netminder equal to it.

But soon, the Steelers had a lifeline with 13 minutes to go when Eric Neiley fired his shot over Bowns' glove and into the net, halving the deficit to one.

Cardiff held their nerve in the final stages and the fans were only able to breathe when Jake Morissette finished the empty netter with 17 seconds to go and the celebrations began.

Report by Elite League Media - www.eliteleague.co.uk

Sunday 8th April
Play Off Final

Cardiff Devils 3
Sheffield Steelers 1
P/Scores: 0-0, 0-2, 1-1
SOG: She 24 – Car 33
PIM: She 6 – Car 6

Sheffield Scoring:
Eric Neiley 1+0
Miika Fransilla 0+1

Cardiff Scoring:
Matt Pope & Andrew Hotham 1+1, Jake Morissette 1+0, Patrick Asselin &Gleason Fornier 0+1

Referees:
Tom Darnell
Mike Hicks
Linesmen:
James Kavanagh
Danny Beresford

Sunday 8th April
Third Place Game

Fife Flyers 2
Nottingham Panthers 8
P/Scores: 1-3,1-3, 0-2
SOG: Fife 27 / Nottm 41
PIM: Fife 0 - Nottm 0

Fife Scoring:
Jim Jorgensen & Carlo Finucci 1+0, Charlie Mosey, Ricards Birzins, Shane Stockton, Chase Schaber all 0+1

Nottingham Scoring:
Zack Phillips & Ollie Betterdige 2+0, Luke Pither, Mark Derlago, Jeff Brown, David Clarke all 1+1, Yann Sauve 0+2, Jordan Kelsall, Josh Tetlow, Steven Lee, Alexander Mokhshantsev, Raphael Bussieres all 0+1

Referees:
Stefan Hogarth
Dean Smith
Linesmen:
Ilia Kisil
Allan Ward

Elite League

Saturday 7th April
Semi Final 1

Fife Flyers 0
Cardiff Devils 4
P/Scores: 0-0, 0-1, 0-3
SOG: Fife 19 – Car 38
PIM: Fife 8 – Car 10

Referees:
Tom Darnell
Stefan Hogarth
Linesmen:
James Kavanagh
Allan Ward

Saturday 7th April
Semi Final 2

Nottingham Panthers 4
Sheffield Steelers 5
P/Scores: 2-1, 2-1, 0-2,
Overtime: 0-1
SOG: Not 36 – She 42
PIM: Not 6 – Shef 10

Referees:
Dean Smith
Mike Hicks
Linesmen:
Ilia Kisil
Danny Beresford

Quarter Finals
1st Leg 30/31 March
2nd Leg 1st April

Belfast 4 – Nottingham 3
Nottingham 5 - Belfast 3
Nottingham win 8-7

Coventry 2 – Cardiff 4
Cardiff 4 – Coventry 3
Cardiff win 8-5

Sheffield 5 – Guildford 2
Guildford 5 – Sheffield 4
Sheffield win 9-7

Fife 1 – Manchester 4
Manchester 1 – Fife 5
Fife win 6-5

Photos from top:
Cardiff Devils celebrate winning the Play Off Trophy

Devils v Fife Flyers in the first semi final

Nottingham Panthers v Sheffield Steelers in the second semi final.
(Photos by Richard Davies – Chud Photography www.smugmug.chud.com)

NIHL North

Match action from the Moralee Division game between Nottingham Lions and Whitley Warriors
(Photo by Richard Davies – Chud Photography)

The season in the Moralee Division went pretty much as expected with the three former EPL teams dominating the leading positions for much of the season.

Billingham Stars actually topped the table after the first weekend of games due to their 11-3 win over Deeside Dragons but, after that, they lost 14 of their next 15 games in league and cup and never troubled the upper reaches again.

Solway Sharks topped the table briefly in September (as, indeed, did Blackburn Hawks) and the Scottish team were the clearly the best of the "old NIHLers" over the course of the season making 4th place their own as early as November.

Telford Tigers led the way for much of the early season but, once the two bigger money teams - Sheffield Steeldogs and Hull Pirates – got into their stride, it soon became obvious that the league title would definitely end up in Yorkshire – either East or South

The Steeldogs led the league table from November through to the end of February and then swapped places with the Pirates a few times - leaving the destination of the title in question right up to the last weekend of the season when, ironically, the two teams played each other home and away.

The Steeldogs won 1-0 at home on the Saturday and then 4-6 away in Hull the following night to secure the title and finish 3 points ahead of the Pirates in the final league standings.

The former NIHL teams all took points off each other, making for a reasonably enjoyable season – albeit bereft of trophies - for most of the teams in the division.

Moralee Division new boys Nottingham Lions struggled - winning just 5 of their 36 league games – but they still did better than bottom team Deeside Dragons who only won two games all season – once against Solihull Barons early on and once against the Lions.

The Dragons had a particularly disastrous campaign, losing head coach and leading player Scott McKenzie back to his old club Telford after just 8 games of the season and then seeing a stream of other players leaving the club once McKenzie was no longer then and as results became increasingly worse.

NIHL North

Moralee Division – Final League Table 2017/18

	P	W	OW	OL	L	PIM	F	A	Pts
Sheffield Steeldogs	36	28	3	1	4	496	191	72	63
Hull Pirates	36	26	3	2	5	434	274	110	60
Telford Tigers	35	26	1	2	6	284	212	77	56
Solway Sharks	35	19	1	1	14	287	172	123	41
Solihull Barons	36	16	5	1	14	702	182	132	41*
Whitley Warriors	36	16	0	4	16	492	135	145	36
Blackburn Hawks	36	13	3	1	19	603	142	145	33
Billingham Stars	35	10	1	2	22	533	155	178	24
Nottingham Lions	36	5	0	3	28	432	84	214	13
Dragons (Deeside)	35	2	0	0	33	804	77	428	4

Top Points Scorers – Moralee Division 2017/18

Player	Team	GP	G	A	Pts	PIM
Matthew Davies	Hull Pirates	29	31	86	117	49
Jason Hewitt	Hull Pirates	29	39	58	97	65
Jason Silverthorn	Telford Tigers	31	43	48	91	16
Bobby Colin Chamberlain	Hull Pirates	28	44	41	85	62
Richard Plant	Telford Tigers	33	18	56	74	26
Chris Sykes	Billingham Stars	33	41	30	71	24
Milan Kolena	Sheffield Steeldogs	35	36	33	69	48
Lee Bonner	Hull Pirates	30	29	35	64	40
James Archer	Hull Pirates	30	27	30	57	44
Deniss Baskatovs	Billingham Stars	33	22	35	57	22
Iain Bowie	Solway Sharks	34	26	31	57	4
Samuel Towner	Hull Pirates	30	20	37	57	14

Top Netminders – Moralee Division 2017/18

Netminder	Team	GP	TOI	SA	GA	Sv%	SO
Dmitri Zimozdra	Sheffield Steeldogs	31	5	739	41	94.45%	5
Denis Bell	Telford Tigers	33	9	751	53	92.94%	9
Brandon Stones	Sheffield Steeldogs	34	7	319	23	92.79%	3
Adam Long	Hull Pirates	19	48	562	47	91.64%	3
Joshua Nicholls	Solihull Barons	20	35	606	53	91.25%	1
Richard Lawson	Whitley Warriors	31	45	951	90	90.54%	2
Mark Turnbull	Whitley Warriors	28	32	402	42	89.55%	2
Stuart Lee Ashton	Blackburn Hawks	31	28	705	76	89.22%	1
Daniel Brittle	Solihull Barons	33	50	695	77	88.92%	0
Mark Watson	Billingham Stars	27	22	577	65	88.73%	3
Calum Hepburn	Solway Sharks	33	23	777	88	88.67%	3

NIHL North

Above: Sheffield Steeldogs celebrate winning the Moralee Division title following dramatic home and away wins over runners up Hull Pirates in the last two games of the season. (Photo by Peter Best Photography)

Matty Davies of Hull Pirates was the Moralee's top points scorer. (Photo by Lois Tomlinson - http://loistomlinson.wixsite.com/photography)

Steeldogs' Dmitri Zimozdra was the top netminder with a 94.45% Save Percentage (Photo by Peter Best Photography)

Peter Best Photography

https://peterbestphotography.pixieset.com/

Twitter: @pbestphotography   Inst: PBPhotoUK

The Telford Tigers team celebrate winning the Moralee Division Play Off title at iceSheffield after a two legged 9-2 win over league champions Sheffield Steeldogs. (Photo by Peter Best Photography.)

NIHL North Division 1 (Moralee) Play Offs 2018

NIHL North Division 1 Play Offs – Final

1st Leg – 31st March 2018	2nd Leg – 1st 2018	Aggregate Score
Telford 6 - Sheffield 0	Sheffield 3 – 2 Telford 2	Tigers win 9-2

NIHL North Division 1 Play Offs – Semi Finals

1st Leg – 24th March 2018	2nd Leg – 25th March 2018	Aggregate Score
Solihull 3 - Sheffield 4	Sheffield 5 – Solihull 2	Steeldogs win 9-5
Telford 5 - Hull 5	Hull 3 – Telford 4	Tigers win 9-8

NIHL North Division 1 Play Offs – Quarter Finals

1st Leg 17th March 2018	2nd Leg 18th March 2018	Aggregate Score
Billingham 3 – Sheffield 4	Sheffield 9 - Billingham 3	Sheffield win 13-6
Hull 12 – Blackburn 1	Hull unable to travel	Hull go through
Whitley 2 – Telford 5	Whitley unable to travel	Telford go through
Solway 4 – Solihull 4	Solihull 5 – Solway 3	Solihull win 9-7

Following highly successful play off weekends in recent years, the format for the Moralee Division play-offs was changed to mirror the more laborious "three round" version that had been played in NIHL South in previous seasons.

The team that finished 1st in the league played the team that finished 8th, 2nd played 7th, 3rdplayed 6th and 4th played 5th in two legs over one weekend and then the winners played semi-finals the weekend after.

The third weekend of play saw the final two teams playing off home and away for the title. The final weekend, however, was somewhat devalued by the fact that both teams qualified for the "final four" north v south weekend at Coventry and many fans thought that the new format was too drawn out.

NIHL North

Laidler Division – Final League Table 2017/18

	P	W	OW	OL	L	PIM	F	A	Pts
Sutton Sting	36	27	1	3	5	495	218	110	59
Widnes Wild	35	23	2	1	9	682	207	82	52*
Hull Jets	36	21	5	0	10	594	243	129	52
Telford Tigers	36	23	2	1	10	702	247	145	51
Altrincham Aces	36	19	3	5	9	866	218	114	49
Sheffield Senators	35	19	2	1	13	939	222	134	44*
Bradford Bulldogs	35	13	1	3	18	777	145	151	32*
Coventry Blaze	35	10	2	3	20	721	149	137	28*
Dragons (Deeside)	34	3	0	1	30	728	95	423	9*
Blackburn Hawks	36	0	1	1	34	617	61	380	3

*Note – Unplayed Games: Hull Jets v Widnes Wild 18.3.18 awarded 0-5 win to Widnes
Dragons v Widnes, Bradford v Dragons & Coventry v Senators all awarded 0-0 - ie point each.*

Laidler Division - Top Points Scorers – 2017/18

Player	Team	GP	G	A	Pts	PIM
Richard Haggar	Hull Jets	31	72	56	128	26
Karol Jets	Telford Tigers	32	43	74	117	44
Callum Bowley	Telford Tigers	34	48	56	104	42
Gowan Beddoes	Hull Jets	30	38	46	84	4
Oliver Barron	Widnes Wild	32	43	39	82	44
Jay Robinson	Hull Jets	30	26	54	80	168
Stuart Brittle	Widnes Wild	33	26	52	78	30
James Smith	Telford Tigers	18	34	44	78	47
Joseph Colton	Sutton Sting	34	30	47	77	20
Scott Morris	Sutton Sting	33	30	41	71	50

Laidler Division – Top Netminders 2017/18

Player	Team	GP	TOI	SA	GA	Sv%	SO
Matthew Croyle	Widnes Wild	28	4	772	50	93.52%	3
Declan Ryan	Altrincham Aces	14	52	690	47	93.19%	2
Philip Pearson	Bradford Bulldogs	22	21	840	58	93.10%	1
Adam Cherry	Altrincham Aces	18	59	133	10	92.48%	3
Phil Crosby	Widnes Wild	15	18	244	22	90.98%	1
Zack Brown	Telford Tigers	20	23	698	64	90.83%	3
Warren Gilfoyle	Sutton Sting	28	38	976	95	90.27%	4
Hayden Laverick	Coventry Blaze	18	34	102	10	90.20%	0
Robert Browne	Sheffield Senators	15	44	370	39	89.46%	0
Ian Thirkettle	Bradford Bulldogs	20	54	799	87	89.11%	1
Dean Bowater	Hull Jets	28	46	963	105	89.10%	3

NIHL North

Above: Sutton Sting celebrate winning the Laidler Division league title
(Photo by Christopher Rastall Photography)

Richard Haggar of Hull Jets was the top points scorer in the Laidler Division for the second season in a row with 72+56=128 in 31 games. (Photo by Fiona Haggar)

Widnes Wild's Matt Croyle was the division's top netminder with a 93.52 Save % (Photo by Geoff White – www.gw-images.com)

NIHL North

Laidler Division Round Up – by Paul Breeze

The 2017/18 Laidler Division was by far the closest competed league in British ice hockey with 6 different teams leading the table over the course of the season with just one point or less separating the top 4 teams at various stages.

Sheffield Senators led the table after the first weekend of play but that was the only time they bothered the upper reaches of the league and they ended up having a poor season by their own standards.

Widnes Wild got off to a flying start and won 6 games on the trot to give player coach Ollie Barron the inaugural NIHL player of the month award and, during this early season high, they beat title favourites Sutton Sting twice at home and did the same with the highly fancied Telford Tigers.

Altrincham Aces had strengthened their team quite considerably and looked likely to do even better than the previous season's 4th place finish. They signed several players from the title winning Blackburn Eagles team and had a very good phase, knocking Widnes off the top of the table and looking good title contenders for much of the winter period.

Telford Tigers had a brief purple patch and kept both Aces and Widnes off the summit for a short period and Hull Jets – having their best season for years, with Richard Haggar, Kieran Beach and Gowan Beddoes monopolising the scoring charts - also topped the table heading into the final quarter of the campaign.

However, once Sutton Sting got into their stride, it seemed almost inevitable that most people's pre-season favourites would go on to win the title. They had games in hand over all the other teams at the top and, once they overtook them, they stayed there until the end of season.

Telford rallied after a poor-ish spell to eventually take the 4th play off spot forcing the Aces down into 5th and second and third became the subject of an off-ice dispute between Widnes, Hull and the EIHA.

The Wild's second visit to Hull in February had to be postponed because the Hull Pirates' team needed to use the Jets' ice time to play their cup semi final. The replacement date of 18th March suggested by the EIHA didn't suit the Jets players and no other date was available before the deadline for playing Laidler Division matches. Widnes claimed the points as Hull hadn't made adequate attempts to fulfil the fixture and these were duly awarded following a league management meeting, handing the Wild second place – on equal points with the Jets.

With the same two teams due to meet in the play off semi-final at Widnes in April and with hardly the proverbial cigarette paper between them, expectations were high on both sides and a thoroughly nail baiting and enthralling match ensued (see following pages for details of Play Off weekend).

NIHL North

If things were close at the top of the table, they weren't too dull at the bottom end either. Regular strugglers Bradford Bulldogs and Coventry Blaze found some new fodder to get their respective teeth into with the arrival of two new teams for the season.

Following the somewhat controversial move to force the Blackburn Eagles team out of their home rink and ultimately out of existence, their place was taken with a Blackburn Hawks development team, made up of mainly young players with a few old heads to guide them, and with a view to giving them regular league experience rather than just the odd "guest shift" that they might otherwise get on the Hawks' Moralee team bench.

This "Hawks 2" team was joined by a "Dragons 2" team from Deeside made up, again, mainly of young players and a notable number of former recreational players as well. The two development teams had some very close-fought and competitive games between the two of them but struggled when it came to facing anybody else.

In a TV interview for "Drop the Puck" early in the season, Hawks 2 captain Joe Charlton set out the objectives for the development team as "to get some experience, score a few goals and try not to get beaten too heavily" and, from rather one sided scorelines at the start of the season, both teams did actually improve a lot as time went by – albeit moreso the Hawks than the Dragons.

Despite finishing bottom of the Laidler table with just 3 points from 36 games, the people in Blackburn must have been happy with the Hawks 2 experiment as they came back for another go at development for the 2018/19 Laidler season. Not so the "Dragons 2", who ,following the relegation of the senior Dragons team from the Moralee Division, ceased to be - with players and resources from both teams joining forces for the new united Dragons campaign.

Matches between Hawks 2 and Dragons 2 were always very highly entertaining encounters.
(Photo by Yorkie Rawcliffe)

NIHL North

LAIDLER DIVISION PLAY OFF WEEKEND
Planet Ice, Widnes

The RTL-sponsored Widnes Wild ice hockey team retained their Laidler Division Play Off title after a sensational 6-3 win in the final against league champions Sutton Sting at Planet Ice Widnes. .

It was the first time that the prestigious play off weekend had been staged in Widnes and the top four teams in the division played out two semi-finals on the Saturday with the two winners meeting on the Sunday.

The Wild had to come from behind in their semi-final game against the Hull Jets, trailing 2-5 at the mid-way point of the game before fighting back to draw 5-5 at the end of the third period and forcing the game into overtime.

The extra 5 minutes of play produced no "golden goal" winner so the tie went to a penalty shoot-out – the first one ever seen at Planet Ice Widnes. The score was tied at one penalty each after three attempts and it actually took 4 more rounds of "sudden death" shots before the two teams could be separated, with the Wild's Shaun Dippnall firing in the winning penalty much to the delight and relief of team-mates and fans alike.

The other semi-final saw Sutton Sting beat Telford Tigers 4-3 to set up a champions v runners up battle for the coveted play off title.

The Wild opened up a two goal lead in the first period but were pegged back with two quick strikes by Sutton early in the second. Despite having to defend for long periods of the game, Widnes made the most of their chances and scored two more before the Sting scored their 3rd goal in the 53rd minute. A goal by the Wild's Stuart Brittle with just 3 minutes left play pretty much settled the game and the win was made certain with an empty net goal by hat-trick man Nick Manning in the dying seconds.

A minute's silence was held before each semi-final game on the Saturday in memory of the casualties from the Humboldt Broncos ice hockey team's bus crash in Canada. A Broncos team flag was signed by all the players over the weekend and raffled off with the proceeds going to the Broncos families fund.

Report by Paul Breeze

**Sunday 15th April
Play Off Final**

**Sutton Sting 3
Widnes Wild 6**
P/Scores: 0-2, 2-1, 1-3
SOG: Sut 52 – Wid 39
PIM: Sut 10 – Wid 14

Full Team Line Ups and Player Stats:
Sutton Sting: Bailey Templar, Simon Butterworth (0+1), Brady Doxey (0+1), Jake Anthony Apsley, Joseph Colton AC, Ryan Johnson (2PIM), James Goodman (0+1), Scott Morris Captain (0+1 2PIM), Stanislav Lascek (3+0 2PIM), Charlie Saunders, Jonathan Williamson (0+1 2PIM), Matt Jeffcock (0+1), David Pyatt AC, Will Curzon, Oliver Mitchell, Nicholas Winters NM, Warren James Gilfoyle NM, Cameron Ross Glasby, Dominic James Martin (2PIM), Elliot Meadows

Widnes Wild: Andrew Turner (1+1 4PIM), Daniel Bracegirdle, Oliver Barron (0+1), Ken Armstrong, Daniel Bullock (1+0 2PIM), Matthew Barlow, Geoff Wigglesworth (2PIM), Lee Kemp AC, Michael Gilbert, Nicholas Manning (3+0) Berwyn Hughes (2PIM), Simon Offord Captain (0+2), Stuart Brittle AC (1+1), Pavel Vales (0+1 2PIM), Thomas McDonald NM, Matthew Croyle NM, Thomas Ratcliffe, Kyle Haslam, Thomas George Jackson (2PIM), Michael Robert Mawer, Shaun Dippnall (0+2)

Referee:
Adam Hands

Linesmen:
Ethan Hardy
Scott Rodger

Laidler Division Play Off Weekend at Planet Ice, Widnes

Top left: Wild Captain Simon Offord receives the Trophy from EIHA Vice-President Chares Dacres
Top right: Wild's Shaun Dippnall fires in the decisive penalty shot in the semi-final against Hull Jets.
Middle: Widnes Wild team celebrate their second play-off title in a row.
Bottom: Match action from the first semi-final between Telford and Sutton.

(All photos by Geoff White – www.gw-images.com)

Saturday 14th April
Play Off Semi–Final 1

Sutton Sting 4
Telford Tigers 3
P/Scores: 1-1, 2-1, 1-1
SOG: Sut 63 – Tel 23
PIM: Sut 56 – Tel 20

Sutton Scoring:
Simon Butterworth (0+1),
Joseph Colton (1+0),
Ryan Johnson (0+1),
James Goodman (0+1)
Scott Morris (2+1),
Stanislav Lascek (1+2)
David Pyatt (0+1)

Telford Scoring:
Karol Jets (1+1),
Callum Kurt Griffin (1+0),
Joseph Aston (0+1),
Daniel Thomason (1+0),
Callum Bowley (0+2),
Liam Preece (0+1)

Match Officials:
Adam Hands – Referee,
Ethan Hardy –
Linesman,
Alice Stanley –
Linesman

Play Off Semi–Final 2

Widnes Wild 6
Hull Jets 5 (PS)
P/Scores: 1-0, 2-5, 2-0,
OT: 0-0, PS: 3-2
SOG: Wid 41 – Hull 37
PIM: Wid 22 – Hull 14

Widnes Scoring:
Oliver Barron (1+1),
Michael Gilbert (0+1),
Nicholas Manning (1+1),
Stuart Brittle AC (1+1),
Pavel Vales (0+3),
Shaun Dippnall (2+0)

Hull Scoring:
Kieran Beach (0+2), ,
Jamie Lewis (0+1),
Gowan Beddoes (2+1),
Richard Haggar (1+2), ,
Jay Robinson (1+0),
Andrew Ward (1+1)

Match Officials:
Richard Fraley –
Referee,
Richard Wang –
Linesman,
Scott Rodger –
Linesman

Coventry Play Off Weekend

BASINGSTOKE BISON WIN NATIONAL CHAMPIONSHIP, COMPLETES TROPHY TREBLE

By Craig Simpson, EIHA Media & Communications

Basingstoke Bison completed a trophy treble in Coventry, adding the NIHL Final Four to their league and playoff titles, beating Telford Tigers 4-0 in the Grand Final.

The National League's first big weekend tournament saw impressive pre-sales for what is a new type of event for many of the clubs and their fans. In the end almost all NIHL 1's 19 sides were represented plus supporters from other clubs around the UK as well as the NIHL2 finalists Oxford and Sutton all getting a weekend hockey fix.

Bison edged out the north league winners Sheffield Steeldogs 3-1 in their Saturday semi final, a huge save from Dean Skinns on a Milan Kolena penalty shot when just a 2-1 game before captain Aaron Connolly added his hat-trick marker into the empty net to seal the win.

Telford's ticket to the dance was stamped courtesy of a 4-1 semi final win over Peterborough Phantoms. Scott McKenzie netted twice while Denis Bell made 14 third-period saves to prevent a Phantoms comeback. Tigers fourth goal, McKenzie's second, was into an empty net 74 seconds from time.

Sunday's final began with Telford's 19+2 bench against Bison only 13+2. However when the puck dropped Basingstoke made light of the numerical disadvantage, a strong forecheck and speedy transition game causing problems for Telford from the off.

Bison capitalised on an early powerplay as Kurt Reynolds beat Denis Bell for the opener at 6.22 before Aaron Connolly bagged his fourth of the weekend before the first break.

The shot count of 13-4 confirmed Basingstoke dominance as Telford's offence just would not or was not allowed to fire.

Another powerplay goal early in the middle frame from Josh Smith – being in the right place at the right time to put home a rebound – widened the gap further. And how did the Bison man celebrate!

Eventual man of the match Ivan Antonov put the seal on the result with a clinical fourth just past the half hour and it was game, set, match and championship to Doug Sheppard's Hampshire outfit.

The final shot count saw Bison hold Telford to just 15 shots on target in the game, testament to the way they shut down one of the most potent scoring teams in the NIHL. The celebrations at the end showed what it meant to everyone in a black Bison jersey.

Sunday 8th April 2018
Play Off Final
Basingstoke Bison 3
Telford Tigers 4

Period Scores:
1-0, 2-1,1-0
Shots On Goal:
Tigers 33 – Phantoms 23
Penalties In Minutes:
Widnes 36 – Aces 24

Tigers Scoring:
Scott McKenzie 2+0, Richard Plant 1+0, Macaulay Holland 1+0,
Jonathan Weaver 0+3, Jason Silverthorn 0+2, Joe Miller 0+1

Phantoms Scoring:
James White 1+0, Ales Padelek 0+1

Match Officials:
Tim Pickett / Stuart Smith
Andrew Cook

Sunday 9th April 2018
D2 Championship Game
Sutton Sting 1
Oxford City Stars 3
Period Scores:
0-0, 0-2,1-1
Shots On Goal:
Sting 41 – Stars 43
PIM: Sting 2 – Stars 8

Sting Scoring:
Stanislav Lascek 1+0, Joseph Colton 0+1

Stars Scoring:
Michael Willock & Joe Edwards both 1+1, Conor Redmond 1+0, Joshua Oliver & Dominic Hopkins both 0+1

Match Officials: Tim Pickett / Stuart Smith / Flynn Sitch-Cunningham

Coventry Play Off Weekend

Saturday 7th April 2018
Play Off Semi Final 1
Telford Tigers 4
Peterborough Phantoms 1
Period Scores: 1-0, 2-1,1-0
Shots On Goal: Tigers 33 – Phantoms 23
Penalties In Minutes: Telford 4 – P'boro 6

Tigers Scoring:
Scott McKenzie 2+0, Richard Plant 1+0,
Macaulay Holland 1+0, Jonathan Weaver
0+3, Jason Silverthorn 0+2, Joe Miller 0+1

Phantoms Scoring:
James White 1+0, Ales Padelek 0+1

Match Officials:
Tim Pickett / Stuart Smith Andrew Cook

Saturday 7th April 2018
Play Off Semi Final 2
Basingstoke Bison 3
Sheffield Steeldogs 1
Period Scores: 0-0, 1-1,2-0
Shots On Goal: Bison 31 – Steeldogs 29
Penalties In Minutes: Bison 6 – Steeldogs 8

Bison Scoring:
Aaron Connolly 3+0, Kurt Reynolds, Ryan
Sutton, Paul Petts, Joshua Smith all 0+1

Steeldogs Scoring:
Milan Kolena 1+0, Thomas Relf, Ashley Calvert
both 0+1

Match Officials: Paul Brooks / Nathan
Carmichael / Flynn Sitch-Cunningham

Match action from the Division 2 North v South Play Off game at the Final Four Weekend. Oxford City Stars beat Sutton Sting 3-1 (Photo by Christopher Rastall Photography)

©Christopher Rastall Photography
NIHL Sport Photography

NIHL Player Awards

NIHL Player of the Month

For the 2017/18 season, the EIHA announced a new series of Player of the Month awards to be presented to a winner in each division, ie NIHL North Moralee & Laidler and NIHL South Britton & Wilkinson - for each month of the season.

The winners were chosen by a panel of dedicated media experts who regularly watch and cover NIHL hockey and the awards were presented to the winning players at the next available home game in each case.

Winner of the inaugural Player of the Month award for the Laidler Division (for October 2017) was Widnes Wild player coach Oliver Barron (Photo by Geoff White – www.gw-images.com)

The month by month winners of the Player awards for all four NIHL divisions are shown below:

	Moralee	Laidler	Britton	Wilkinson
September	Iain Bowie *(Solway Sharks)*	Ollie Barron *(Widnes Wild)*	Ryan Watt *(Streatham IHC)*	Stephen Woodford *(Haringey Huskies)*
October	Matty Davies *(Hull Pirates)*	Warren Gilfoyle *(Sutton Sting)*	Frantisek Bakrlik *(Bracknell Bees)*	Shaun Yardley *(Pbr Phantoms 2)*
November	Sam Towner *(Hull Pirates)*	Gowan Beddoes *(Hull Jets)*	Jordan Lawday, *(Cardiff Fire)*	Richard Facey, *(Solent Devils)*
December	Scott McKenzie *(Telford Tigers)*	Zack Brown *(Telford Tigers 2)*	Aaron Connolly *(Basingstoke Bison)*	Kamil Kinkor *(Oxford City Stars)*
January	Chris Sykes *(Billingham Stars)*	Dominic Martin *(Sutton Sting)*	Michael Farn *(Streatham IHC)*	Lukas Smital *(Slough Jets)*
February	Dmitri Zimozdra *(Sheffield Steeldogs)*	Ryan Kemp *(Bradford Bulldogs)*	Owen Griffiths *(P'boro Phantoms)*	Grant Bartlett *(Chelms Chieftains)*
March	Denis Bell *(Telford Tigers)*	Nathan Britton *(Sheffield Senators)*	Aaron Nell *(Swindon Wildcats)*	Aaron Craft *(Basingstoke Buffalo)*

The overall Player of the Season awards for each division were presented at their respective Play Off weekends and are shown on the following page.

NIHL Player Awards

Moralee Division Player of the Season 2017/18
Dmitri Zimozdra of Sheffield Steeldogs
(Photo by Peter Best)

Wilkinson Division Player of the Season 2017/18
Michael Farn of Streatham Redhawks
(Photo by Rick Webb)

Laidler Division Player of the Season 2017/18
Richard Haggar of Hull Jets
(Photo by Geoff White www.gw-images.com)

Wilkinson Division Player of the Season 2017/18
Richard Facey of Solent Devils
(Photo by Kevin Slyfield)

NIHL South Division 1 (Britton) Review
by Chris Randall, NIHL South Editor

Well here we are again, 12 months on as we look back on another season of NIHL South hockey.

There was one big difference however, as with the collapse of the former English Premier League, (EPL) the league took on a much changed look. Additions to the League included Basingstoke Bison, Bracknell Bees, Swindon Wildcats and Peterborough Phantoms all coming in from the now defunct EPL.

From last year's NIHL 1 sides, Streatham RedHawks, London Raiders, Invicta Dynamos and Milton Keynes Thunder all returned and a team set up as Cardiff Fire took the brave decision took step up to the much improved division.

South1 lost perennial Champions Chelmsford Chieftains as they stepped down a level, dropping to South 2 for the 2017/2018 season, much to the dismay of several clubs, and they were joined by Oxford City Stars - along with Bracknell Hornets. These clubs cited increased competition and higher budgets from the former EPL teams as the main reasons for them dropping to NIHL South 2.

Well starting at the top , Doug Sheppard had an EPL quality side at the ready in Basingstoke. With some big name players at his disposal such as Czechs Tomas Karpov, Roman Malinik and Yaroslavl Cesky along with Brits Dan Davies and Aaron Connolly the talent was there to see. Built around a strong defence with Dean Skinns and Dan Weller-Evans in net, the goaltending was in safe hands.

Defensively experienced blue liners Joe Baird, long time Bison Kurt Reynolds and Dan Scott showed a sold back end. Ably supported with Stuart Mogg and Dan Lackey who had shown considerable improved seasons with Lackey stepping up from the South 2 side Buffalo. Elliot Dewey returned after some time at Invicta Dynamos.

Winning the League on the final weekend of the season in dramatic fashion wasn't in the script as Peterborough Phantoms pushed them all the way. However, despite wining silverware question marks remained over the future of the rink with its building suffering from structural issues.

Second place slot was filled by Peterborough Phantoms who were nip and tuck all the way with eventual champions Basingstoke Bison right up to the final weeks. The results couldn't have been closer with the series neck and neck and it came down to goal difference as the decider as all other stats couldn't separate them.

Phantoms Head Coach Slava Koulikov again proved his credentials, as his side wasn't stacked with depth and lots of big name signings . However he got the team playing a very defensively minded style, which in some quarters of the league was deemed "Boring". However, if it didn't entertain some, it certainly got results even if it didn't get the pulse racing for opposition fans .

Another solid side with names such as Euan King in net, a defence with former Elite leaguer Leigh Jamieson and forwards Nathan Salem, long time Phantom James Ferrara supportered by some good young players, they had a very good side. Imports Ales Padelek, and veteran Darius Pilskauskas added scoring and experience .

It was just everyone's view they wasn't exciting to watch. They ended the year with no trophies which could be seen as a disappointment. Had they had some of that attacking flair such as Basingstoke had they could have maybe pipped them to the post.

Swindon Wildcats continue to grow. As they flourished in the new look NIHL South 1. Owner Steve Nell had son Aaron Nell back as Player-Coach with a majority of the previous year's team back as well.

Some say they had some good depth. With import former Cardiff Devils forward Maxim Birbrear and Czech big strong Jan Korstal they were a very entertaining team to watch. They liked to skate and attack and had a nice mix of youth and experience. Tomas Rutkis played on a two way with Elite side Cardiff Devils and impressed. Floyd Taylor had a breakout season with Joe Haseldine and Jordan Kelsall adding tenacity.

Former Cardiff Devil Chris Jones came in and added depth. With experience in the shape of Phil Hill, Neil Liddiard experience was a-plenty. Sam Zajac and Stephen Whitfield oozed the passion in the side as did Sam Bullas who would drop em with anyone.

A stellar year in net for Renny Marr saw them captured two trophies at season's end. With crowds in four figures and the commercial side growing each year the Wildcats future is purring along nicely.

Well, after the big four dropping down from the EPL with Basingstoke, Swindon, Peterborough and Bracknell most assumed that they would be the top 4. Tell that to one Essex based outfit - as London Raiders upset the form book to clinch 4th place in the standings!

Sean Easton left Chelmsford Chieftains and joined up with returning Head Coach Alan Blyth to address the 2017/2018 Season.

A majority of last year's side returned. Long-time Raider Michael Gray donned the pads in net once again for what was his 9th season for Romford/London Raiders in addition to a season with the now defunct Spitfires NIHL 2 side. He was a standout last season, facing a tonne of shots , performing admirably.

Equally good, Euan King returned but left at the deadline to join hometown team Peterborough and back up Zach Grandy-Smith saw a little action behind the experienced two.

Defence was solid with returnees John Connolly, Julian Smith and shot blocker Andy Munroe all back. A host of Chelmsford Chieftains joined with Sean Barry and Calum Wells added.

Peterborough Phantoms were close all season but lost out in the end to Basingstoke Bison
(Photo by Paul Young - Peterborough Images / Nene Digital)

London Raiders take on Bracknell Bees in their new Sapphire Ice And Leisure Centre home in Romford
(Photo by John Scott)

Up front the Chieftains exodus continued as Speedy Brandon Ayliffe, Oliver Baldock, Jake Sylvester and Olegs Lascenko all joined the Essex rivals despite the fact they play in separate leagues now.

Familiar names included sniper Juraj Huska, and fellow Slovak Marek Nahlik . To add depth, two way centre Matt Turner and Jj Pitchley and Captain Tom Davis all donned the Gold and blue.

Fiesty Alan Lack rejoined from Basingstoke Bison and suffered a horrendous facial injury after taking a puck to the face. Surprisingly he returned to just a few weeks later, wearing a full face protection.

These were the attributes that all the players displayed in droves as the passion from the players went through to the fans.

The biggest news of course was moving back to Romford in their brand new facility. The crowds flocked back to watch the team with several sellout signs going up on the doors. They last played in the town some 5 years ago before the move to Lee Valley.

The team probably overachieved for the season in most people's eyes and no doubt they will look to continue to move forward this coming season.

Looking up at London Raiders were the Bracknell Bees. A team that dropped from the EPL and most assumed they would dominate the top of the league. They had a great start, but somewhere along the line the wheels fell of ever so slightly as they went two months without a league win.

A host of talented names included net minders Alex Mettam and Danny Milton backed up by a defence that included experienced Carl Graham, Tom Avery and young Harvey Stead. Two way deals saw Joshua Tetlow get Champions League hockey under his belt with Nottingham Panthers. Import defence man Jan Bendik was a feature on the blue line - the Czech native having been solid on the blue line for the Bees in recent years.

Forwards had plenty of youth: Ben and Josh Ealey-Newman brothers, Josh Martin and Danny Ingoldsby in the side speed and tenacity wasn't an issue. Experienced Matt Foord, Calum Best, Alex Barker was supported well with gritty players such as Scott Spearing who would be Player coach. Along with Shaun and younger brother Carl Thompson the side looked solid enough.

Additions included Steve Osman who would later leave for Invicta at the deadline. George Norcliffe left Streatham for the Hive. So, a fairly decent looking side. 5th place was what they finished up with so the season should be seen as a major disappointment, given the roster they had.

Streatham RedHawks' Head Coach Jeremy Cornish looked to continue to build on the High Road in South London. A few familiar names didn't return as he had a re-jig in order to compete with a now much improved League.

The former Wightlink flavour was evident as net minder Marty Colclough, Nate Gregory, Brendan Baird ,Jordan Gregory, Alex Sampford, Dan Rose , Ryan Webb and Aiden Doughty all camped out on SW16.

Streatham RedHawks v Invicta Dynamos (Photo by fusional.co.uk. Tw: @Fusionators)

Milton Keynes Thunder v Swindon Wildcats (Photo by Lucy McGill – Lucy McGill Photography)

Utility player Adam Wood and speedy forechecking penalty killing supreme Joe Allen was what came back from the old guard.

The side had an import in Andreas Siagris who hailed from Burnaby, BC in Canada.

Former Streatham legends Tony and Alec Goldstone were synonymous with Streatham so young Alec Goldstone was the latest name to be added after stepping up from the juniors. Another to step up was net minder Brett Shepherd who impressed enough also.

Big name additions over the summer saw former MK Lighting players Forward Adam Carr and standout defender Michael Farn added to the roster. They certainly made an impact . Farn recievimg "Player of the year" award from the League. With Carr's experience proving invaluable . They was a hit on the High Road and its great news they are both returning for the 2018/2019 season.

6th place was a disappointment but, given the improved competition in the League Streatham beat the top sides, Swindon being one. Their cup exploits went well especially the League Cup going undefeated but falling at the end. All in all a season that they made improvements.

Can Coach Cornish raise the bar another level ? . Time will tell....

Towards the lower end of the table were Milton Keynes Thunder. Head Coach Lewis Clifford returned with a host of players to compete with some tough opposition.

Net minder Tom Annetts was back and veteran Mark Woolf. In defence Alex Whyte, Nidal Phillips and Lewis Christie returned to form the nucleus. Veteran Greg Randall, Rupert Quincy and Ross Green also on the back end , showed a solid enough blue line corps.

Offensively Tom Carlon was added from the Lightning, along with gritty Grant McPherson. Not one to shy away from the feisty side of the game. Tom Mboya, Connor and Harrison Goode all gave the side a familiar look about it.

Ross Bowers was a lynchpin for them, with youth in Michael Stratford added, speed came in the shape of diminutive Jamie Line and Rio Grinnel-Parke .

They had some credible results even against some of the former EPL sides. However, they were always up against it, struggling to compete with the budgets some of the top end teams. They were always in a different world but they did finish above Invicta Dynamos - so that must be seen as a plus.

Invicta Dynamos had really a horrid season. Players leaving, been shown the door (Calum Fowler) or one thing or another they struggled to make inroads in an improved League structure. After being used to being at the top end of the standings for so many years, being near the bottom wasn't familiar surroundings for the Kent outfit.

As ever Head Coach Kev Parrish continued in the hot seat. Last year's returnees included Net minder Damien King, John Dibble returned full time after helping out last season when they had an injury crisis. Fans favourite Tommy Ralph, Captain Arran Strawson, and Harrison Lillis all committed to the season too.

Forwards back included Calum Fowler who was later released, Mason Webster who had a stellar year, showing true battling qualities and his younger brother came on board and displayed similar traits.

The players leaving moving on stage was very evident early on. Bobby Chamberlain had a job offer back in his native North East so he packed his bags before he had barely settled. Last year's standout forward Ashley Jackson rejoined the side late on after starting the season with Basingstoke Bison.

Tom Long came out of his lengthy sabbatical (the former Wightlink Raider, and Chelmsford Chieftain having not iced since 2012) but he hardly played.

Finally, Czech import Jaroslav Cesky came in to replace outgoing Adam Rehak who just didn't cut it this time around in a better league. Steve Osman was added at the deadline too.

So the theme was one of a very unsettled roster with no continuity at all - a season to forget, really. No doubt Coach Parrish will have a lot of work to do going forward .

Finally propping up the League were Cardiff Fire. They came in and took the brave decision to compete in a league where they were always going to find the going tough.

Head Coach Mark Cuddihy had plenty of talented youth at his disposal but even sprinkled with a bit of experience, the season was a hard one. Just a few points over the course of the season says it all, really, and credit to them as they battled hard all season long.

They got some sponsors on board, have a nice new rink and committed players but the quality was sadly lacking in a season to forget. Hardly surprising that they have taken the decision to not play a team in South 1 this season - a wise move if they want to progress.

So there you have it: the top half, the middle pack and the struggling bottom three. That was the 2017/2018 Britton Division season in NIHL South 1.

NIHL South

South 1 (Britton) Division – Final League Table 2017/18

	P	W	OW	OL	L	PIM	F	A	Pts
Basingstoke Bison	32	26	2	0	4	306	158	60	56
Peterborough Phantoms	32	23	4	2	3	286	159	69	56
Swindon Wildcats	32	18	4	4	6	485	150	92	48
London Raiders	32	16	2	1	13	504	121	106	37
Bracknell Bees	32	13	3	2	14	703	137	125	34
Streatham	32	13	1	1	17	838	114	110	29
Milton Keynes Thunder	32	6	3	6	16	407	74	120	25
Invicta Dynamos	32	6	3	4	19	714	88	137	22
Cardiff Fire	32	0	0	2	29	628	41	223	3

Britton Division – Top Points Scorers 2017/18

Player	Team	GP	G	A	Pts	PIM
Tomas Karpov	Basingstoke Bison	32	29	38	67	28
Aaron Nell	Swindon Wildcats	29	23	35	58	26
Ivan Antonov	Basingstoke Bison	29	16	40	56	22
Frantisek Bakrlik	Bracknell Bees	23	30	23	53	117
Maxim Birbraer	Swindon Wildcats	31	15	38	53	44
Nathan Salem	Peterborough Phantoms	31	21	31	52	12
Shaun Thompson	Bracknell Bees	26	22	30	52	4
Aaron Connolly	Basingstoke Bison	31	27	22	49	20
Darius Pliskauskas	Peterborough Phantoms	31	21	26	47	12
Daniel Davies	Basingstoke Bison	29	21	25	46	4
Michael Farn	Streatham	29	12	34	46	42

Britton Division - Top Netminders 2017/18

Player	Team	GP	TOI	SA	GA	Sv%	SO
Adam Long	Peterboro Phantoms	14	33	277	22	92.06%	1
Dean Skinns	Basingstoke Bison	32	1	666	54	91.89%	5
Euan King	Peterboro Phantoms	19	42	661	54	91.83%	3
Euan King	London Raiders	4	42	661	54	91.83%	3
Renny Marr	Swindon Wildcats	31	58	755	65	91.39%	2
Tom Annetts	MK Thunder	28	21	1077	93	91.36%	2
Damien King	Invicta Dynamos	28	21	1225	106	91.35%	0
Michael Gray	London Raiders	25	59	872	76	91.28%	0
Matthew Colclough	Streatham	28	38	987	94	90.48%	4
Daniel Weller-Evans	Basingstoke Bison	32	59	61	6	90.16%	1

NIHL South

Above: The South 1 Britton Division's top overall points scorer Basingstoke's Tomas Karpov and highest goal scorer, Frantisek Bakrlik of Bracknell Bees. Karpov hit 29+38=67 in 32 games whereas Bakrlik took only 23 games to score 30 goals. Had he not sat out 117 PIM in those 23 games and, indeed, not picked up an 18-game suspension at the end of February, his end of season total would undoubtedly have been far higher....

Basingstoke Bison netminder Dean Skinns was the Britton Division's best individual netminder with a 91.89 Save % over 32 games. (Both photos by Kevin Slyfield Photography)

NIHL South Division 1 Play Offs – by Chris Randall

Well after the exciting 32 game season, the Top 8 out of the 9 teams in NIHL South 1 (Britton) Conference headed for the End of Season Playoffs with technically 3 weekends of post season action, culminating in a Final 4 style weekend at Coventry Sky dome at the beginning of April.

As with previous years, this was seeded 1st v 8th, 2nd v 7th, 3rd v 6th and 4th against 5th and some mouth watering ties lay ahead.

Starting off, League Winners Basingstoke Bison took on the defending Play off Champions Invicta Dynamos. This was always, on paper, likely to be one way traffic given that Coach Kev Parrish and his Invicta Dynamos team had failed in several attempts to even get close to Doug Sheppard's Basingstoke outfit home or away. This was simply a case of getting the job done.

However, Dynamos - with nothing but pride and players maybe playing for jobs next year - gave a good account of themselves in the end to at least try and compete with the far stronger Bison.

Runners up in the League by the narrowest of margins (goal difference), the Peterborough Phantoms had a local derby as Milton Keynes Thunder battled the Fenland side. Thunder have added some quality players over the last few seasons and are no longer an easy win, having taken points through the season of some of the former EPL sides.

So this was an interesting set of matches. Despite some close action between both sides, Slava Koulikov's experience as a non-playing Coach paid off with the Phantoms triumphing over the two legs to advance.

Swindon Wildcats took on Jeremy Cornish and the Streatham RedHawks. This could have potentially been a banana skin for the 'Cats and Player coach Arron Nell. However, they brushed aside the challenge comfortably in the second leg after the RedHawks battled bravely for half the weekend, but came up short against an strong Swindon side as Swindon won comfortably.

London Raiders' great season (4th Place) in the League had them up against 5th place Bracknell Bees. It's fair to say London were defiantly Bracknell's bogey side and the Playoffs were no different. With a packed house at Sapphire Ice and Leisure the Essex outfit had a tough battle. It produced some close exciting hockey as London managed to beat the Bees over the two legs to complete the final four from the NIHL South 1.

The second round of matches had Basingstoke Bison to face London Raiders and Swindon Wildcats taking on Peterborough Phantoms in the last of the home and away ties before the Winners of each Conference headed for Coventry to face their Northern counterparts .

So Basingstoke Bison v London Raiders again was a exciting few matches as London matched the Bison for large parts, Bison eventually coming through however to set up

NIHL South

a showdown with the Sheffield Steeldogs (NIhl North League Champs) at Coventry the following week.

Swindon Wildcats and Peterborough Phantoms battled over the weekend with the exciting attacking play from the Wildcats against what most across the League described as boring defensive trapping it up hockey of the Phantoms.

Swindon actually won both games home and away but fell foul of he NIHL rules about player eligibility. They incorrectly allowed an Under 18 player to ice in the home game - which they won 4-2 but this game was eventually awarded 0-5 to Peterborough as the player concerned hadn't played the required 25% of league games to be able to take part in the play offs. Obviously, this was merely a gesture to give a young home-grown player a bit of big game experience rather than a cynical attempt to gain an unfair advantage by using a season player from somewhere else - which is what this rule was designed to prevent - but that's the rule and, as with Chelmsford Chieftains who did a similar thing last season, the infringement had to be punished.

This meant that the Phantoms went through to the two legged Britton Division play off final against Basingstoke and both those teams qualified for the "Final Four" national play off finals at Coventry as well.

The two games were as close as the league campaign had been for the two rivals and after 1-1- draw in Peterborough on the Saturday, Basingstoke won 2-1 on the Sunday to take the S1 Play Off title.

Phantoms lost 4-1 to NIHL North Play off winners Telford Tigers in the first national semi final on the Saturday while Basingstoke beat NIHL North Moralee Division winners Sheffield Steeldogs 3-1 in the second semi.

This set up a fascinating north v south final as Basingstoke took on Telford, coming out 4-0 winners to secure the treble of S1 league, S1 Play Off and National Play Off titles.

NIHL South Division 1 Play Offs – In Figures
NIHL South Division 1 Play Offs – Final

1st Leg – 31st March 2018	2nd Leg – 1st April 2018	Aggregate Score
Peterborough 1 – Bas'stoke 1	Basingstoke 2 – Peterboro' 1	Bison win 3-2

NIHL South Division 1 Play Offs – Semi Finals

1st Leg – 24th March 2018	2nd Leg – 25th March 2018	Aggregate Score
London R 4 – Basingstoke 7	Basingstoke 3 – Raiders 0	Bison win 10-4
Swindon 4 – Peterborough 2 *(Match awarded 5-0 to Peterborough as Swindon iced ineligible player)*	Peterborough 4 – Swindon 6	Phantoms win 9-6

NIHL South Division 1 Play Offs – Quarter Finals

1st Leg 17th March 2018	2nd Leg 18th March 2018	Aggregate Score
Streatham 0 – Swindon 2	Swindon 4 - Streatham 2	Swindon win 6-2
Bracknell 5 (Lon) Raiders 6	Lon Raiders 4 – Bracknell 2	Raiders win 10-7
Basingstoke 6 – Invicta 0	Invicta 1 – Basingstoke 7	Basingstoke win 13-1
MK Thunder 2 – Peterborough 7	Peterborough 4 – MK 2	Peterborough win 11-4

South 2 (Wilkinson) Division – Final Table 2017/18

	P	W	OW	OL	L	PIM	F	A	Pts
Oxford City Stars	26	22	1	0	3	397	223	55	46
Solent Devils	26	22	0	1	3	464	164	58	45
Bracknell Hornets	26	21	0	1	4	553	159	93	43
Chelmsford Chieftains	26	20	0	0	6	619	186	74	40
Peterborough Phantoms	26	15	2	0	7	570	144	84	36
Guildford Phoenix	26	14	1	1	10	518	111	87	31
Slough Jets	26	7	5	0	14	618	104	153	24
Bristol Pitbulls	26	10	0	1	14	406	103	104	22
Cardiff Fire	26	10	1	0	15	748	97	138	22
Haringey Huskies	26	8	1	1	16	470	93	162	19
Basingstoke Buffalo	26	6	0	4	16	490	78	158	16
Invicta Mustangs	26	5	2	1	18	614	75	161	15
Swindon Wildcats	26	6	0	1	19	419	85	158	13
Lee Valley Lions	26	1	0	2	22	325	70	207	5

Wilkinson Division - Top Points Scorers 2017/18

Player	Team	GP	G	A	Pts	PIM
Richard Facey	Solent Devils	26	43	42	85	52
Kamil Kinkor	Oxford City Stars	23	38	37	75	20
Alex Murray	Solent Devils	26	20	48	68	10
Lukas Smital	Slough Jets	21	20	47	67	34
Steven Fisher	Bracknell Hornets	26	29	37	66	58
Andrew Campbell	Solent Devils	26	26	31	57	20
Grant Bartlett	Chelmsford Chieftains	15	28	27	55	76
Cameron Bartlett	Chelmsford Chieftains	23	27	28	55	129
Ross Brears	Chelmsford Chieftains	23	19	32	51	24
Joshua Oliver	Oxford City Stars	25	30	21	51	26
Shaun Yardley	Peterborough Phantoms	20	11	39	50	52

Wilkinson Division – Top Netminders – 2017/18

Player	Team	GP	TOI	SA	GA	Sv%	SO
Christian Cole	Solent Devils	24	36	599	44	92.65%	3
Sonny Phillips	Chelmsford Chieftains	23	57	619	53	91.44%	4
Andrew Leckie	Bristol Pitbulls	21	1	151	13	91.39%	2
Mark Duffy	Oxford City Stars	24	8	229	20	91.27%	2
Milan Ronai	Oxford City Stars	23	50	320	28	91.25%	4
William Sanderson	Bracknell Hornets	18	1	465	43	90.75%	2
Jacob Stoodley	Guildford Phoenix	21	37	502	47	90.64%	1
Billy Cyril Cook	Chelmsford Chieftains	25	59	207	21	89.86%	3
Ross Miller	Bristol Pitbulls	22	0	894	91	89.82%	0
Chris Douglas	Slough Jets	22	47	1155	118	89.78%	1
James Richardson	Bracknell Hornets	26	0	463	50	89.20%	0
Daniel Ashley Lane	Peterboro Phantoms	23	39	704	81	88.49%	2

Oxford City Stars – Wilkinson Division Champions 2017/18 – Photo by Paul Foster

While missing out on the league title – admittedly by just one single point - the Solent Devils swept the board with the top player stats in every department. Richard Facey (below left – photo by Dave Chapman) was top goalscorer with 43 and top points scorer with 85. Alex Murray got the highest assists with 48 and Christian Cole (below – right by Kevin Slyfield) was the top netminder with a 92.65 Save %.

NIHL South Division 2 (Wilkinson) Round Up
by NIHL South Editor Chris Randall

The 2017/2018 NIHL South 2 Season or, as it was known, the "Wilkinson" Division became that much bigger over the off season in 2017. With the additions of three former South 1 teams joining, it became a 14-team League with a 1 home, 1 away format to give a 26 League game schedule.

The additions of former South 1Champions Chelmsford Chieftains, Oxford City Stars and Solent Devils came at a very late stage of the summer. Other plans had already been made for the South 1 league set up with those three clubs doing a U-turn at the last minute to join the lower South 2 instead, citing Budgets and competitiveness as the sole reasons for the change of heart.

Everyone expected the former Division 1 clubs to be top dogs and run away with it, however, a lot of the clubs lower down the table surprised a lot of the bigger budget sides.

The League was won by the narrowest of margins - by just a single point - with Oxford City Stars the winners on 46 points. Solent Devils pushed them all the way finishing on 45 points with the last few games being pivotal. Bracknell Hornets also challenged all season long.

Stars had great depth with likes of All-Star Defence man Dom Hopkins, long time Stars player Darren Elliot as well as many other South 1 calibre players in their side they were tough to beat. They lost just 3 games all season long.

Down on the South Coast, in the league's smallest rink, Alex Murray Player-Coach for the Solent Devils had some talented players who gave their all and ended in style at season's end (Playoffs) more on that later . They had Richard Facey firing on all cylinders as well as great netminding from Chris (Chico) Cole. Import Drew Campbell helped the younger players and added scoring. Again, they lost just a few games.

The same went for Danny Hughes and the Bracknell Hornets . Some great players, they looked like likely League Champs at one stage only to lose a couple of key Championship 4 pointers games late on.

Former South 1 Champs Chelmsford Chieftains had a rocky spell and lost 6 games in all, settling for 4th place. The Bartlett brothers Cam and Grant dominated their scoring.

Peterborough Phantoms 2 also had a wobble after a great start again looking like they may crack the top 3 but a determined effort wasn't enough to challenge the top.

The surprise package of the season without doubt was the new boys on the block. The Guildford Phoenix had some great young players and they over-achieved with their first ever South 2 side. Upon entering the league, they turned heads and got some great results. Winning more than they lost was a commendable effort and former Guildford Flames player Andrew Hemmings' first season as Player-coach was a successful one.

NIHL South

Czech Lukas Smital and his Slough Jets had to play most of the season in a temporary sized small rink, constructed on the main rink's car park. Finishing below new side Guildford should be seen as a disappointing season.

Richie Hargreaves - owner, Player-Coach, minibus driver and Mr Do It All continued to keep the Bristol Pitbulls flying in their home from home at Oxford. Seems like a lifetime ago since the Frogmore Street rink closed for Student housing. Hope is on the horizon however for a new rink in the City, which would be just reward for his family who have kept the team going for a long time. 22 points and 10 wins was enough for mid table.

Cardiff Fire , Haringey Huskies and Basingstoke Buffalo all occupied the next three spots in the standings, separated by just a few points and then came a youthful Invicta Mustangs and Swindon Wildcats 2 nearby.

Bottom spot with 5 points went to Lee Valley Lions as they managed to sneak just the 1 win and two overtime losses.

So that was the 2017/2018 NIHL South 2 Season as it was. The top half all fairly close, the middle pack and the bottom separated from 13 points to 24. Some viewed the season as success. Others, on the other hand, felt that the top 4 should have been in the League above.

Chelmsford Chieftains v Invicta Mustangs in NIHL South Division 2 (Wilkinson) action at Chelmsford
(Photo by Steve Sutherland – www.icecoldphoto.co.uk)

Sunday 22nd April
Play Off Final

Chelmsf'd Chieftains 1
Solent Devils 6
P/Scores: 0-0, 1-1, 0-5
SOG: Che 33 – Sol 29
PIM: Che 30 – Sol 35

Chelmsford Scoring:
Michal Oravec 1+0
Ross Brears 0+1

Solent Scoring:
Mark Pitts 2+1, Mitchell Murray & Alex Murray 1+1, Alex Trendall & Richard Facey 1+0, Mason Wild 0+2, Drew Campbell 0+1

Referee:
Andrejs Korsaks
Linesmen:
Justin Lalonde
Oliver Finch

Saturday 21st April
Semi Final 1

Oxford City Stars 3
Chelmsf'd Chieftains 5
P/Scores: 0-2,2-0, 1-3
SOG: Oxf 56 – Che 35
PIM: Oxf 8 – Che 10

Referee: David Good
Linesmen:
Emma Sanders
Oliver Finch

Semi Final 2

Solent Devils 6
Guildford Phoenix 1
P/Scores: 1-0, 2-0, 3-1
SOG: Sol 31 – Gui 28
PIM: Sol 16 – Gui 16

Referee:
Andrejs Korskas
Linesmen:
Nick Hayman
Justin Lalonde

Quarter Finals
(Played 14th / 15th April)

Bracknell 1 – Guildford 2
no ice time at Guildford
Guildford win 2-1

Bristol 3 – Oxford 4
Oxford 10 – Bristol 1
Oxford win 14-4

Peterboro 4 – Chelms 9
Chelms 8 – Peterboro 1
Chelmsford win 17-5

No ice time at Slough
Solent 6 – Slough 3
Solent win 6-3

Photos on this page courtesy of Kevin Slyfield Photography.
Official Bracknell Bees Photographer
See more at: *https://www.flickr.com/photos/juniorbeesicehockey*
email: *kevin.slyfield@gmail.com*

Photos from top: The minute' silence before the Oxford v Chelmsford semi final / Match action from the Solent v Guildford semi final / Solent Devils, Play Off Champions (All by Kevin Slyfield).

NIHL South Division 2 (Wilkinson) Play Offs 2017/18
By Chris Randall

Well after a summer of uncertainly with the League structure with the former EPL clubs joining the League, once the dust had settled the League Management Committee set about devising the Playoff structure across the whole of the NIHL.

The Wilkinson Division (NIHL South 2) mirrored the South 1 (Britton) Division and had the top 8 teams qualify for the end of season play offs, with 1st v 8th, 2nd v 7th, 3rd v 6th and 4th v 5th, with the winners facing each other at the Quarter Final stages. The difference was that the semi finals and final would be played as one off games at Bracknell over a special finals weekend.

Oxford City Stars faced off against a team that share their home rink as Bristol Pitbulls still playing on the road for home games at Oxpens Road . They put up a stiff fight, however Oxford City Stars superior strength in depth an more experienced roster triumphed over the two legs to advance to the Semi finals .

Chelmsford Chieftains came up against Peterborough Phantoms (2) and Chelmsford won comfortably over the two legs to advance to the next round.

The next two opponents had issues regarding ice time availability as new boys Guildford Phoenix where unable to get home ice with the Elite League Flames taking priority. A suggested Wednesday slot was quashed by their opponents Bracknell Hornets as player unavailability the reason. So a one-off tie at the Hive in Berkshire settled the tie. It went the way of the surprise package Guildford who had pushed them hard all the way to claim a famous victory and set up a Semi Final showdown.

The final quarter final games pitted Alex Murray's Solent Devils against Lukas Smital and his Slough Jets. Again with the Jets playing most of the season in their temporary under sized rink whilst the Hanger was being refurbished. They (Slough) could only possibly get ice playing with closed doors to the public. Again, a 1 off match at Solent Devils was arranged and Devils came out on top to face Guildford at the Semi Final stage.

So the semi final action had Solent Devils take on Guildford Phoenix. A slow start by Solent kept it close. However as the game wore on Devils finally woke up and found their groove coming out on top.

The other Semi Final was a "Clash of the Titans" so to speak as League Winners Oxford City Stars took on Chelmsford Chieftains. Oxford having already won the League title was looking to advance to the final and go for a Double. Their Essex opposition had other ideas as Chelmsford and in particular the Bartlett brothers were in no mood to let a disappointment of 4th place stop them getting to Sunday's final .

So Sunday's final saw Solent Devils take on Chelmsford Chieftains. Again, a slow start by the Devils but, as time wore on and they relaxed after taking a lead, they tightened their grip on the game to prevail 6-1 winners and become 2017/18 NIHL South 2 (Wilkinson) Play off Champions.

Swindon Wildcats celebrate winning the Autumn Cup (Photo by Ben Callaghan)

NIHL Autumn Cup - Season 2017/2018

Autumn Cup – Final

1st Leg – 9th March 2018	2nd Leg – 16th March 2018	Aggregate Score
Basingstoke 1 – Swindon 3	Swindon 4 – Basingstoke 2	Wildcats win 7-3

Autumn Cup - Semi Finals

1st Leg – Dates As Shown	2nd Leg – Dates As Shown	Aggregate Score
11/1/18 Swindon 3 – Peterboro 3	19/1/18 Peterboro 3 – Swindon 4	Swindon win 7-6
26/1/18 Basingstoke 4 – Hull 3	7/2/18 Hull 1 – Basingstoke 4	Basingstoke win 8-4

Qualifying Groups

Group A	P	W	OW	OL	L	F	A	Pts
Basingstoke Bison	4	3	0	1	0	54	14	7
Peterborough Phantoms	4	2	1	0	1	30	18	6
Sheffield Steeldogs	4	0	0	0	4	52	5	0

Group B	P	W	OW	OL	L	F	A	Pts
Swindon Wildcats	4	3	1	0	0	66	14	8
Hull Pirates	4	2	0	1	1	180	15	5
Telford Tigers	4	0	0	0	4	42	6	0

Cup Round Up by Chris Randall

Every season there are several cup competitions across the NIHL. This year the 2017/2018 season was no different with Autumn Cup and League Cup taking place.

We start with the Autumn Cup which, ironically, was played out with the latter stages being finalised in more like the winter months rather than the autumn as the competition finished in February.

Featuring sides from the North and South conferences . Two groups with Group "A" featuring Basingstoke Bison, Peterborough Phantoms and Sheffield Steeldogs while Group "B" featured Swindon Wildcats, Hull Pirates and Telford Tigers.

In each group the teams had 4 matches , playing 1 home and 1 away . The winners of each group and runners up went on to play Semi Finals home and away with the Winners of that then playing home and away in the Final .

Swindon Wildcats meant business as they finished with a 3 wins and an overtime win to end the group stage with 8 points and go unbeaten .

Semi Finals action saw a 1st leg draw 3-3 at the Link Centre against Peterborough. The 'Cats followed that up with a 4-3 win in the Fens against the Phantoms to advance to the Final winning closely on aggregate 7-6.

They met Basingstoke Bison . Wildcats established a narrow 1st leg 3-1 lead on the road. Swindon wrapped up with a 4-2 success at home in Wiltshire to win 7-3 on aggregate and become 2017/2018 NIHL Autumn Cup Champions on the 16th February .

Following on from their Autumn Cup success the Swindon Wildcats added the League Cup trophy to their cabinet as the season reached it latter stages.

After 12 matches that doubled up as League/Cup Swindon finished with 8 wins, 2 overtime wins and 2 losses.

Quarter finals and they dispatched London Raiders with relative ease with a 14-2 aggregate win in early January.

They then went onto face the Telford Tigers at the semi final stage and send them packing with their tails between their legs. Swindon gaining an 8-4 aggregate win.

Saving the best till last at the Finals and Wildcats triumphed 6-4 over Sheffield Steeldogs in mid- April to end the season with two trophies in the cabinet.

NIHL National Cup - Season 2017/2018

NIHL National Cup – Final

1st Leg – 11th April 2018	2nd Leg – 15th April 2018	Aggregate Score
Sheffield 2 – Swindon 2	Swindon 4 – Sheffield 2	Wildcats win 6-4

NIHL National Cup - Semi Finals

1st Leg – Dates As Shown	2nd Leg – Dates As Shown	Aggregate Score
14/2/18 Swindon 3 - Telford 3	20/2/18 Telford 1 – Swindon 5	Swindon win 8-4
2/2/18 Sheffield 3 – Hull 2	3/2/18 Hull 1 – Sheffield 3	Sheffield win 6-3

NIHL National Cup – Quarter Finals

1st Leg – Dates As Shown	2nd Leg – Dates As Shown	Aggregate Score
20/1/18 Solway 2 – Sheffield 6	21/1/18 Sheffield 4 – Solway 2	Sheffield win 10-4
14/1/18 Streatham 2 Telford 5	20/1/18 Telford 4- Streatham 4	Telford win 9-6
6/1/18 Blackburn 3 – Hull 4	7/1/18 Hull 12 - Blackburn 3	Hull win 16-6
13/1/18 Swindon 8 – London R 0	14/1/18 Raiders 2 – Swindon 6	Swindon win 14-2

Qualifying Groups

Group 1	P	W	OW	OL	L	PIM	F	A	Pts
Solway Sharks	8	5	1	0	2	76	41	28	12
Blackburn Hawks	8	4	0	0	4	130	35	41	8
Billingham Stars	8	2	0	1	5	151	29	36	5

Group 2	P	W	OW	OL	L	PIM	F	A	Pts
Hull Pirates	7	4	1	0	2	176	27	30	10
Sheffield Steeldogs	8	3	0	1	4	224	29	36	7
Peterborough Phantoms	7	3	0	0	4	84	38	28	6

Group 3	P	W	OW	OL	L	PIM	F	A	Pts
Streatham	8	8	0	0	0	213	35	17	16
London Raiders	8	3	1	0	4	161	32	23	8
Invicta Dynamos	8	0	0	1	7	193	15	42	1

Group 4	P	W	OW	OL	L	PIM	F	A	Pts
Swindon Wildcats	12	8	2	0	2	208	46	35	20
Telford Tigers	12	6	1	1	4	169	38	33	15
Basingstoke Bison	12	4	1	1	6	120	37	41	11
Bracknell Bees	12	2	0	2	8	213	35	47	6

PLAYER INTERVIEW
Andy Pickles

Over the years many Brits have taken up the game of Ice Hockey and enjoyed many years enjoying and giving back to the sport. A name that most Basingstoke Beavers/Bison , Wightlink Raiders and Peterborough fans will remember is that of Andy Pickles.

Now currently looking to get back into playing, albeit at Rec level, any rec side would be happy to have the former GB international in their side and that's exactly what the Badger is aiming for .
Nihl South Editor Chris (the Badger) Randall caught up with him to talk about his time in the game.

Here's what Andy had to say ......

CR. At what age did you start skating ?

I started skating lessons aged 8, learnt to skate as a figure skater first, taught how to use edges, power skating and things a hockey player may not learn before holding a stick.

CR. What are your earliest memories of playing?

Earliest memories of playing were at the now long gone Bournemouth Ice Rink, a run down, barely standing building. My first game was a blur but I remember the coach saying "get in your lines and warm up" and I had no idea what that meant! My first away game was at the old Streatham rink and we got hammered and one of their players threatened to stab me after the game. I mentioned this to Tony Blaize and he said it could well have been him who said that!

CR. Your dad was involved in the British game for many years with the now defunct BIHA. Your dad must have had some influence in you skating and taking up the game at an early age?

Regarding my Dad, i was playing before he got involved in any way. I went to Bournemouth aged 8 only because I saw an advert in our local paper! When he ran the British Ice Hockey Association, I was already playing at a high standard at Basingstoke for the Beavers so I would like to say that, even though he pretty much ran the sport in the 90's, I got where I got off my own back and hard work. I wouldn't ever want any favours or to get things because of someone who had a high profile in the sport. He was basically a free taxi from the age of 8 till about 17 which I'm very grateful for - after that, time my career and his were very separate.

CR. Over the years, what would be a main highlight for you?

I was fortunate to have enjoyed a long career, which I'm very proud of. A few highlights are winning the league with Basingstoke, winning cups with Peterborough and the Isle of Wight. I got voted into the BNL Allstar team with Bracknell Bees in 1996, played for GB u21s, captained the GB Lions team once (a team solely of British trained players), had many tours with various GB age groups but my number one highlight was playing for GB senior team in 2001 in the World Championships in Slovenia. I got 7 caps for the senior team and this was at a time when the team was very much influenced by 'Canadian' Brits and I think there was possibly a 50/50 split with them and British born and trained players, such as Tony Hand, Longstaff, Dixon, Weaver, Tait was a real honour.

CR. You played at the highest level in the UK game in the SuperLeague. Being the only Brit in the Bracknell Bees at one time. What are your memories of that time and do you think it was a move to soon for the British game ? ..

'The Superleague' I remember it so well, really mixed feelings on that. Personally, I developed massively being the only Brit on the Bracknell Bees team. Limited game time but training with these guys 3/4 times a week improved me more than I realised at the time. The speed, the skill level, game management were all something I wasn't used to and I had to accelerate my game in order to try to compete with these guys.

So many other British lads who weren't as lucky as me could have been given the chance in that league but it was basically millionaire owners wanting a hobby and - allegedly - a decent tax write off.

I don't think it's so much the Superleague franchise to blame but a combination a Sky Sports who pumped tons of cash into the sport that went straight into players pockets (they then dropped Ice Hockey again almost immediately), many of which were poor second rate imports who never would have earned anywhere near as much in another league but got very lucky. I blame the Superleague for isolating itself from IHUK and not looking at the bigger picture and taking an interest in junior development/coaching kids. Here we are some 20 years later and nothing has really changed it seems.

CR. You became Team owner and Coach in later years with the Wightlink Raiders on the Isle of Wight . What do you remember about that time in your career and your time on the sunny Isle ? ...

My time on the Island was something I will treasure. I'd had enough of travelling, being away from home, and at the end of my second season at Peterborough I had lost a bit of love for the game. The money wasn't really improving and I didn't love the game like I should have done with the amount of time I spent playing. I was about 27/28 and in my prime and something told me I couldn't just stop playing. I had heard about the Island, the team, the characters, the fans involvement. I had heard a lot of good things so I called Eric Giden in the summer and explained I was ready for a new challenge without the pressures I had played at – or so I thought!!

The Island was a life changer. I loved every second and it re-kindled my love for the game. I wanted to give back something and try to help pass on some of what I had learnt over the years. The fans there are amazing. I trained hard, played at a level better than I had expected and got a move back to Basingstoke Bison after about 10 years away. This led to my GB call up and I'm very proud to be the only player to represent GB senior team while technically being a Raider!

We built up the crowds and got the schools involved. I ended up owning, coaching the team and if you look at it now and how myself and Colesy got Matt Cote, Rob Lamey, Crombs, Adam Carr, Adam Brittle, Bairdy, we had an unbelievable team for a couple of seasons. That is also very much a highlight: how I helped bring that team and success to the fans and the Island. I still can't believe there is no rink there, that's a crime on the Island. I miss the Island, the people but the memories will never go.

CR. After calling time playing, what have you been up to the last few years ? ....

I played a few games for Basingstoke Buffalo aged 43 last season, did ok, scored a few goals, coaches Beere and Skins were brilliant! Looking to play a few rec games now, as you know, Badger, so with your help we can try to do it all again!!!

James Ions photo by Leonie Roberts Photography (www.leonierobertsphotography.com)

MEET THE REF: James Ions

In our regular feature "Meet the Ref" NIHL South Editor Chris (the Badger) Randall caught up with stripey James Ions who despite only been officiating a short time, he has climbed the ladder quickly establishing himself as a great linesman and referee. Here's how James' introduction to the world of Ice hockey came about:

CR: When did you first learn to skate ?

JI: I first learnt to skate at 13 years old, after watching a game in the old rink at the Wales National Ice rink in Cardiff.

CR: Did you play juniors or senior hockey at all when starting out ?

JI: I played at U14 and U16 level in Juniors before leaving the sport. After a few years away I restarted playing at Recreational level. After a sensational beer league record I tried out for Cardiff's ENL division 2 team and managed a grand total of 12 seconds ice time during my half season there. It was probably at this point I decided I wanted to officiate.

CR: At what age did you become an official ?

JI : I started officiating at 22 years of age when I finished up playing. Five years in and I haven't looked back.

CR: And how or who convinced you to become a stripey ?

JI: I would say I convinced myself. I always wanted to be at a higher level in the sport and I would never have made it to any level as a player. As an official I'm involved in professional hockey 2-3 times a week and I've worked at international level. This is more than I ever I imagined when starting out and I'm excited to learn and progress further.

NIHL South

CR: Officials come in for an awful lot of criticism and abuse. Do you hear it or do you learn to block it out ?

JI: During the game I don't hear a thing, I think you're too focused and block out the noise behind you. What we do see is social media abuse, which is horrible. It's not acceptable and shouldn't happen.

CR: Have you got a favourite official you like working a game with ?

JI: I couldn't list a favourite, because there's so many guys out there that have helped me in different ways. Some officials are fun to work with, some are serious and others are tough on you for your own development. That really is the beauty of it, everyone is different and it makes for a great team.

CR: Did you have anyone you idolised or looked to as a role model in the officiating scene ?

JI: No -not at all. I never thought I'd ever be an official, I always wanted to play but my playing skill set bought me to officiating, ha ha! I do admire the way some officials operate during game and off the ice and I try to build that into my game.

CR: What do you think of the current set up of officials in the U.K. ?

JI: If you'd asked this question a few years ago, it may have been a completely different answer but right now it's thriving. The standard is as good as it can be and the development structure is amazing. It makes for exciting times and a very bright future.

CR: What can be done to move it forward even further ?

JI: To keep moving forward we have to 'buy in' to the development and procedures put in place. If we trust the processes then it will be a great success.

CR: What have been your career highlights to date ?

JI: Too many to list, to be honest. First ENL game, first EPL game, first Elite League game. Gaining an international licence, getting a promotion on my international licence. My first international tournament in Denmark and my first senior international game. I didn't imagine achieving any of this and I look forward to adding to the list as we next speak.

I never imagined getting this far but I haven't come this far to stop now. I'd like to officiate all the domestic finals, be involved the Champions Hockey League and advance further at international level.

Our thanks to James Ions for taking the time to talk to us at Ice Hockey Review.

Women's Hockey Round Up

Bracknell Queen Bees won their 7th WEL title in a row – going unbeaten all season with 19 wins and 1 draw in their 20 games (Photo by Barry Beresford)

Women's Elite League – Final League Table 2017/18

Team	GP	W	D	L	F	A	+/-	PIM	Pts
Bracknell Queen Bees	20	19	1	0	119	26	93	108	39
Guildford Lightning	20	12	3	5	73	46	27	179	28*
Solihull Vixens	20	12	1	7	78	60	18	154	25
Kingston Diamonds	20	5	6	9	37	53	-16	250	16
Streatham Storm	20	3	1	16	33	80	-47	175	7
Sheffield Shadows	20	2	2	16	33	108	-75	96	5*

Women's Elite League – Top Points Scorers 2017/18

Player	Team	GP	G	A	Pts	PIM
Christine Newman	Bracknell Queen Bees	19	29	13	42	28
Katie Henry	Solihull Vixens	19	32	9	41	18
Louise Adams	Guildford Lightning	17	22	11	33	6
Jessica Urquhart	Solihull Vixens	18	10	18	28	6
Natalie Aldridge	Bracknell Queen Bees	19	8	19	27	0
Saffron Fern Allen	Solihull Vixens	19	14	13	27	4
Rachel Cartwright	Bracknell Queen Bees	18	21	5	26	20
Emily Harris	Bracknell Queen Bees	15	15	8	23	4

Women's Elite League – Top Netminders 2017/18

Netminder	Team	GP	TOI	SA	GA	SA%	SO
Holly Louise Steeples	Kingston Diamonds	17	51	430	29	93.26%	0
Samantha Bonathan	Bracknell Queen Bees	19	0	336	26	92.26%	3
Alexandra Barrow	Guildford Lightning	17	59	295	23	92.20%	2
Michelle Franklin	Solihull Vixens	17	55	609	52	91.46%	0
Samantha Bolwell	Kingston Diamonds	9	8	237	21	91.14%	0
Ruth Cattell	Streatham Storm	18	58	853	76	91.09%	1
Maisie Gilbert	Sheffield Shadows	9	54	245	26	89.39%	0
Phoebe Shavelar	Guildford Lightning	12	0	158	21	86.71%	1
Jessica Kinghorn	Solihull Vixens	2	0	59	8	86.44%	0
Tamara Donaghue	Sheffield Shadows	17	3	528	76	85.61%	0

Women's Hockey Round Up

Swindon Top Cats won the WPL title and promotion back up to the WEL after just one season away
(photo by Flyfifer Photography - www.flyfifer.co.uk)

Women's Premier League – Final Table 2017/18

Team	P	W	D	L	F	A	+/-	PIM	Pts
Swindon Topcats	12	11	1	0	85	7	78	42	23
Chelmsford Cobras	12	8	1	3	62	37	25	58	17
Milton Keynes Falcons	12	8	0	4	57	26	31	107	16
Kingston Diamonds	12	5	1	6	36	47	-11	92	11
Bracknell Firebees	12	5	1	6	58	52	6	75	11
Widnes Wild Women's Team	12	1	2	9	28	57	-29	110	4
Nottingham Vipers	12	1	0	11	14	114	-100	75	2

Women's Premier League – Top Points Scorers 2017/18

Player	Team	GP	G	A	Pts	PIM
Rebecca Da Cova	Swindon Topcats	10	19	17	36	2
Rebecca Osman	Swindon Topcats	11	16	18	34	6
Tereza Plankova	Chelmsford Cobras	12	20	8	28	20
Rachel Piotrowski	MK Falcons	12	16	11	27	8
Jennifer Bolton	Chelmsford Cobras	12	19	5	24	6
Margeurite Laffitte	Bracknell Firebees	10	7	12	19	2
Sarah-Jane Fletcher	Swindon Topcats	11	2	16	18	8
Monica Petrosino	MK Falcons	9	12	6	18	6
Lucy Anna Beal	Bracknell Firebees	6	6	9	15	0
Reagan Downing	Kingston Diamonds	11	9	6	15	20
Claire Fay	Bracknell Firebees	11	10	5	15	8
Rebecca Inker	Swindon Topcats	11	9	6	15	2

Women's Premier League – Top Netminders 2017/18

Netminder	Team	GP	TOI	SA	GA	SA%	SO
Kayliegh Doyle	MK Falcons	12	38	288	26	90.97%	3
Stephanie Drinkwater	Widnes Wild Womens	10	30	459	48	89.54%	1
Charlotte Cook	Kingston Diamonds	10	54	345	38	88.99%	0
Summer Cramer	Nottingham Vipers	11	45	761	92	87.91%	0
Cherry Hambelton	Chelmsford Cobras	11	45	270	37	86.30%	2
Meryia Throop	Bracknell Firebees	12	30	364	52	85.71%	1

Women's Hockey Round Up

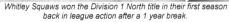
Whitley Squaws won the Division 1 North title in their first season back in league action after a 1 year break.

Squaws' Stephanie Towns was the N1 top scorer with 21+9 in 7 games.

National Division 1 North	P	W	D	L	F	A	+/-	PIM	Pts
Whitley Squaws N1	8	5	2	1	40	19	21	56	12
Blackburn Thunder	8	4	1	3	27	16	11	38	9
Telford Wrekin Raiders N1	8	3	2	3	22	29	-7	64	8
Solway Sharks Ladies	8	3	0	5	28	39	-11	34	6
Sheffield Shadows	8	2	1	5	21	35	-14	85	5

National Division 1 North – Top Points Scorers 2017/18

Player	Team	GP	G	A	Pts	PIM
Stephanie Towns	Whitley Squaws	7	21	9	30	4
Teresa Robinson	Whitley Squaws	7	8	14	22	10
Megan Gourlay	Solway Sharks Ladies	7	9	10	19	4
Hazel Wilson	Sheffield Shadows	7	16	2	18	35
Abigail Rawcliffe	Blackburn Thunder	8	12	2	14	8
Katherine Lyttle	Telford Wrekin Raiders	5	6	5	11	4

National Division 1 North – Top Netminders 2017/18

Netminder	Team	GP	TOI	SA	GA	SA%	SO
Tegan Jenna Lavery	Blackburn Thunder	8	0	284	16	94.37%	2
Jessica Kinghorn	Whitley Squaws	7	0	219	19	91.32%	1
Emma Bevan	Sheffield Shadows	7	57	322	30	90.68%	0
Rebekah Scott	Solway Sharks Ladies	8	58	302	39	87.09%	0
Jodie Alderson	Telford Wrekin Raiders	7	0	214	29	86.45%	0
Rachel Rawson	Sheffield Shadows	5	0	35	5	85.71%	0

graham@flyfifer.co.uk

flyfifer.photography

@flyfiferphoto

Women's Hockey Round Up

The Basingstoke Bison women's team won the S1 title by a single point. Invicta's Lucy Gruber (above, right – photo by Flyfifer Photography) was the S1 leading points scorer by far and also iced 20 times for the Mustangs in NIHL South as well.

Division 1 South	P	W	D	L	F	A	+/-	PIM	Pts
Basingstoke Bison Ladies	16	11	2	3	76	29	47	148	25*
Streatham Storm	16	11	2	3	64	30	34	148	24
Cardiff Comets	16	8	2	6	62	38	24	82	18
Swindon Topcats	16	6	6	4	55	41	14	125	18
Invicta Dynamics	16	8	2	6	72	74	-2	119	18
Coventry Phoenix	15	5	3	8	56	53	3	74	13
Oxford Midnight Stars	16	6	1	9	58	64	-6	68	13
Solent Amazons	16	3	2	11	16	55	-39	84	8
Peterborough Penguins	16	2	4	10	39	114	-75	78	7*

Division 1 South – Top Points Scorers 2017/18					
Player	Team	GP	G	A	Pts	PIM
Lucy Gruber	Invicta Dynamics S1	14	53	8	61	22
Katerina Lossnitzer	Oxford Midnight Stars S1	8	29	8	37	0
Jodie Attrill	Basingstoke Bison Ladies S1	15	27	9	36	4
Parris Moore	Streatham Storm S1	16	19	8	27	12
Jennifer Ball	Cardiff Comets S1	8	18	5	23	2
Rosanne Adey	Coventry Phoenix N1	14	17	4	21	4
Hannah Byrom	Basingstoke Bison Ladies S1	15	16	5	21	39
Aniko Gaal	Basingstoke Bison Ladies S1	14	8	13	21	2
Sharon Khan	Peterborough Penguins N1	15	12	8	20	6
Jessica Sprules	Swindon Topcats S1	12	15	5	20	6

Division 1 South – Top Netminders 2017/18					
Netminder	Team	GP	TOI	SA	GA	SA%	SO
Stephanie Wicken	Streatham Storm	14	35	407	18	95.58%	5
Phoebe Shavelar	Solent Amazons	12	40	295	17	94.24%	2
Samantha Fleming	Cardiff Comets	10	0	102	7	93.14%	1
Katherine Robinson	Basingstoke Bison Ladies	15	20	180	14	92.22%	1
Geraldine Park	Basingstoke Bison Ladies	14	10	186	15	91.94%	2
Courtney Jade Newitt	Swindon Topcats	14	30	455	40	91.21%	0
Mackenzie Whilding	Cardiff Comets	15	30	318	30	90.57%	1

Women's Hockey Round Up

The Bracknell Ice Bees celebrate beating the Kingston Diamonds in the Under 16s National Final

Women's Trophy Weekend at IceSheffield, 19th & 20th May 2018

Featuring:
- Womens Elite League Play Offs (Semi Finals & Final)
- Women's Premier League Play Offs (Semi Finals & Final)
- Womens National League Play Offs (North & South and promotion game)
- Womens Under 16 National Championship (winners of U16 north v U16 south)

Saturday 19th May 2018:
D1 semi final 1: Whitley Bay Squaws 4 – Streatham Storm 3
D1 semi final 2: Basingstoke Bison Ladies 1 - Blackburn Thunder 5

Women's Premier League semi final 1: Swindon Top Cats 2 – Kingston Diamonds 0
WPL semi final 2: Chelmsford Cobras 1 Milton Keynes Falcons 5

WEL semi final 1: Bracknell Queen Bees 8 – Kingston Diamonds 2
WEL semi final 2: Guildford Lightning 2 - Solihull Vixens 5

Sunday 20th May 2018:
D1 final: Whitley Bay Squaws 7 – Blackburn Thunder 4
(Squaws are promoted to the WPL for the 2018/19 season)

WPL Final: Swindon Top Cats 1 – Milton Keynes Falcons 2

U16 Final: Bracknell Ice Bees 6 v Kingston Diamonds 0

WEL Final: Bracknell Queen Bees 7 – Solihull Vixens 1

Scottish National League

Dundee Comets secured the SNL title after a 6-6 draw with Paisley Pirates in the last game of the season.
(Photo by Al Goold)

Above Left: Dundee Comets' John Dolan was the SNL's top points scorer (Photo by Al Goold)
Above Right: Moray Typhoons' netminder Craig Johnstone had the SNL's top SA%, while Kirkcaldy Kestrels'
Craig Douglas had the best GAA (Both photos by Scott K Marshall - @skm1963)

SCOTTISH NATIONAL LEAGUE – FINAL TABLE 2017/18

Team	GP	W	L	D	GF	GA	PTS	GD
Dundee Comets	20	16	2	2	186	60	34	126
Paisley Pirates	20	16	2	2	148	43	34	105
Kirkcaldy Kestrels	20	16	4	0	184	58	32	126
Edinburgh Capitals	19	14	5	0	127	65	28	62
Aberdeen Lynx	20	12	8	0	123	71	24	52
Kilmarnock Storm	19	9	10	0	89	101	18	-12
Moray Typhoons	20	9	11	0	86	101	18	-15
Dundee Tigers	20	8	12	0	75	98	16	-23
North Ayr Wild	20	2	18	0	24	141	4	-117
Kilmarnock Thunder	18	2	16	0	47	197	4	-150
Solway Stingrays	20	2	18	0	64	218	4	-154

SNL Top Points Scorers – 2017/18

Player	Team	GP	G	A	Pts	PIM
JOHN DOLAN	Dundee Comets	19	31	35	66	20
CONOR DUNCAN	Kirkcaldy Kestrels	18	37	27	64	22
RICHARD THORP	Paisley Pirates	20	25	34	59	28
JOHN GORDON	Dundee Comets	20	23	31	54	6
MARC CRUTE	Paisley Pirates	20	19	33	52	26
JOEL GAUTSCHI	Edinburgh Capitals	16	23	28	51	16
SCOTT JAMIESON	Kirkcaldy Kestrels	18	21	23	44	40
GARRY SIMPSON	Kirkcaldy Kestrels	19	19	25	44	16
CALLUM HILL	Dundee Comets	17	11	33	44	12
IAIN MALCOLM	Aberdeen Lynx	18	16	27	43	12

SNL - Top Netminders 2017/18 by Goals Against Per Game Average (GAA)

Netminder	Team	GP	SOG	GA	Mins	Sa%	GAA
CRAIG DOUGLAS	Kirkcaldy Kestrels	15	137	19	447	86.13	2.55
MATTHEW MICHIE	Dundee Comets	20	503	57	1070	88.67	3.2
ANDREW LITTLE	Kirkcaldy Kestrels	14	264	28	520	89.39	3.23
CRAIG CHALMERS	Aberdeen Lynx	20	574	65	1105	88.68	3.53
CRAIG MALLINSON	Edinburgh Capitals	16	502	60	935	88.05	3.85
THEO KYNOCH	Dundee Tigers	15	488	50	728	89.75	4.12
CRAIG JOHNSTONE	Moray Typhoons	9	419	38	491	90.93	4.64

SNL - Top Netminders 2017/18 by Save Percentage (Sa%)

Netminder	Team	GP	SOG	GA	Mins	Sa%	GAA
CRAIG JOHNSTONE	Moray Typhoons	9	419	38	491	90.93	4.64
THEO KYNOCH	Dundee Tigers	15	488	50	728	89.75	4.12
ANDREW LITTLE	Kirkcaldy Kestrels	14	264	28	520	89.39	3.23
CRAIG CHALMERS	Aberdeen Lynx	20	574	65	1105	88.68	3.53
MATTHEW MICHIE	Dundee Comets	20	503	57	1070.	88.67	3.2
CRAIG MALLINSON	Edinburgh Capitals	16	502	60	935	88.05	3.85

Scottish National League

Dundee Comets celebrate winning the SNL League, Play Off and Scottish Cup treble

Scottish Cup Final - Played at Kirkcaldy: 21st April 2018
Dundee Comets 4 – Paisley Pirates 2

Semi Finals	
Kirkcaldy Kestrels 8 - Dundee Comets 9 (4-6, 2-5)	Paisley Pirates 9 – Aberdeen Lynx 7 (6-2, 7-1)

Second Round - Played Various Dates			
Solway Sharks 6 Kirkcaldy Kestrels 15 (9-3, 3-6)	Dundee Comets 12 Kilmarnock Storm 6 (8-4, 4-2)	North Ayr Wild 2 Paisley Pirates 11 (8-0, 2-3)	Aberdeen Lynx 14 Moray Typhoons 6 (5-9, 5-1)

Preliminary Ties: Kilmarnock Thunder 14 – Solway 15 (11-3, 12-3),
Edinburgh Capitals 7 – Kirkcaldy Kestrels 9 (3-5, 4-4)
Dundee Tigers 4 – Dundee Comets 19 (3-11, 8-1
)

NL Play Off Final – Played at Kirkcaldy, 8th April 2018
Dundee Comets 9 – Kirkcaldy Kestrels 2

Semi Finals – Played at Kirkcaldy, 7th April 2018	
Dundee Comets 8 – Aberdeen Lynx 1	Kirkcaldy Kestrels 8 – Paisley Pirates 5

Quarter Finals - Played Various Dates			
1st v 8th: Dundee Comets 21 Dundee Tigers 1 (1-12, 9-0)	4th v 5th: Edinburgh Capitals 6 Aberdeen Lynx 9 (3-1, 8-3)	3rd v 6th: Kirkcaldy Kestrels 15 Kilmarnock Storm 2 (1-8, 7-1)	2nd v 7th: Paisley Pirates 13 Moray Typhoons 2 (12-1, 2-1)

Para Ice Hockey

Kingston Kestrels - British Para Ice Hockey League Champions 2018
Left to Right: Ian Houliston, Tony King, James Morris (behind), Simon Berry (in front), Sarah Coles (from sponsors Irwin Mitchell solicitors), Dave Parker, Matthew Woollias, Dave Blakeston, Matt Clarkson (Photo by Paul Woollias)

British Para Ice Hockey League – Final Standings 2018	P	W	D	L	F	A	Pts
Kingston Kestrels	8	8	1	0	56	5	15
Manchester Mayhem	8	4	2	4	34	25	10
Cardiff Huskies	8	4	1	3	25	24	9
Peterborough Phantoms	8	2	2	4	12	28	6
Sheffield Steelkings	8	0	0	8	3	48	0

The Kingston Kestrels retained their league title in impressive style and repeated the feat that they had achieved last year in going through the whole season unbeaten. This time around, however they did not finish with a 100% record as they could only manage a 2-2 draw in their last home game of the season against Manchester Mayhem.

The first game of the season saw the Kestrels trounce the Mayhem 1-9 at Widnes back in April and that was the only goal that the Kingston team conceded until the very end of the season when they let in two at home to Cardiff in an 8-2 win and then those two to Manchester in their last two games, although by then the title had been long done and dusted.

The top four teams qualified for the play-off weekend where the Mayhem would be looking to defend they title that they won last year in Hull. The play offs were due to be held at Planet Ice rink in Widnes over the weekend of 29th & 30th September and were, unfortunately, too late to be included in this year's Yearbook. However, you will be able to find out what happened on the BPIHA Facebook page...

2018 BRITISH PARA ICE HOCKEY LEAGUE
facebook   www.facebook.com/britishparaicehockey

Raiders v Basingstoke at the new Sapphire Ice and Leisure Centre at Romford (Photo by John Scott).

The new curling rink at the Flower Bowl in Barton near Preston (Photo by Alex Varty)

Cambridge Ice Rink at the end of August 2018 (Photo by David Johnson Photographic)

New Rink News

The best news as far as new rinks during the 2017/18 season was the opening of the new Sapphire Ice and Leisure Centre in Romford back in February.

Following on from the closure of their original Rom Valley Way home of 26 years back in 2013, the Romford Raider teams had been based some 13 miles down the A12 at Lea Valley for five years, playing under the name of London Raiders while waiting for the promise of a replacement facility to come to fruition.

That dream was finally achieved on 3rd February 2018 when the Raiders played Cardiff Fire in a NIHL South S1 Britton match at the new venue, winning 5-2.

The first league goal at the new rink was scored by Cardiff's Jackson Price after 14.37 and the first home goal followed shortly after at 17.40 from Olegs Lascenko.

Barton, near Preston:

The next new ice facility to open in Britain actually opened in August but, disappointingly to most readers of this tome, will not be featuring ice hockey or even ice skating.

The "Flower Bowl" at Barton - up the A6 from Preston - is a new mixed entertainment leisure complex attached to the highly popular Garden Centre. It has 3-screen cinema 8-land bowling alley, crazy golf course, gold simulators, restaurants and cafes and a 4-lane ice sheet for curling.

Although there are twenty or more curling rinks in Scotland, it is actually only the second purpose-built curling rink in the whole of England – the other being the Fenton's rink in Tunbridge Wells, which opened in 2004.

Having not been to visit yet, we asked the nice people at Barton Grange and they gave us the following technical bits and bobs: *"The Curling Rink at The Flower Bowl is a single ice pad split into four curling sheets. There are walkways around the edge but not dividing each sheet. The full size of the rink is 45m x 19m. The facility is for all ages and abilities to enjoy and is fully wheelchair friendly."*

*****

Now: there are numerous announcements being made all the time about plans for new leisure developments which COULD include a new ice rink – most of which never materialise. If every new ice rink that had been announced over the past 30 years or so had actually opened, we'd all have one each by now so, instead of chasing rainbows, we are going to stick with the new rinks that we know a bit more about...

Cambridge:

As things stand, it looks as if the next new ice rink to open will be in Cambridge, where works are well under way on the new venue. It was originally due to open in summer 2018 but progress was hampered by the discovery of 194 unexploded WW2 grenades on the site.

There are hopes that the rink will now open during 2019. The Cambridge Leisure and Ice Centre will have a 56mx26m ice pad 340 seats and an overall spectator capacity of 600. It will be home to the Cambridge University ice hockey teams and the capacity suggests that NIHL hockey would likely follow as well.

Leeds:

On to another rink now where building work has definitely started but progress seems to be rather slow.

The new Silver Blades, as was - now Planet Ice - rink in Leeds near to the Elland Road football stadium has been dogged by delays ever since it was first announced back in 2009. There were numerous planning delays and then geological problems caused by old industrial works under the site. Then, when work did finally get under way in 2017 the structure was damaged by high winds. Construction work was suspended and the planned opening date was put back – again. We are told tentatively

Bristol:

Ongoing plans for a replacement rink in Bristol have not yet come to fruition. Bristol Pitbulls Press Officer Graham Goodman gave us this update:

"In April 2017, South Gloucestershire Council approved plans that included an ice rink for a development beside a major shopping complex in the north of city. However, due to a previous legal challenge on the expansion of that shopping complex, those plans had to be reviewed by Westminster."

"This delay exposed the development to risk from other delays and so it proved. The national election was called preventing Westminster from making any judgements. Once that was over, the Grenfell disaster understandably became the sole focus of the department whose responsibility it was to review the development plans. And then the company who were due to operate the indoor ski slope went out of business. All this meant that the developer missed their deadline to start developing by the end of 2017."

"The good news for 2018 is that modified plans have been submitted, approval of which is expected to be a formality given the success of the original plans. That would mean a likely completion date in time for the 2019-20 season. Ten years to the day since the Bristol Pitbulls played their first league game and seven years since they played that first game as a nomadic team."

More Great Books Available By Mail Order From The Same Publisher

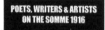

www.icehockeyreview.co.uk

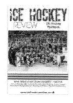  

MORE GREAT ICE HOCKEY BOOKS

 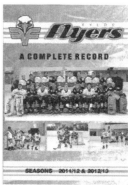 

Hockey Yearbook Back Issues Also Available

Available by mail order from www.poshupnorth.com, Amazon, icehockeyreview.co.uk and other quality outlets

www.icehockeyreview.co.uk